Dear
Thanks
fun, friendship &
meals together -
xo
Rick

UNWRAPPED

Integrative Therapy With Gay Men

... the Gift of Presence

THIS GEM OF A BOOK is a profoundly transformative and rivetingly engaging "master class" in working psychotherapeutically with gay men both to empower them so that they can become the most and the best of who they were meant to be and to free them up so that they can realize their dreams.

On one level, *Unwrapped* is a sobering and achingly authentic story about the loneliness, isolation, shame, self-hatred, and fear that gay men often experience as they struggle to live in a world in which everyone (themselves included) has some degree of internalized homophobia; on another level, however, this tenderly and lovingly crafted book is an uplifting and inspirational story about how a good therapy experience—replete with magical moments of attunement and connection between client and therapist—can facilitate the "coming out" of a man who has been "hidden in" his entire life.

With his eye always on the therapeutic goal of helping his clients live from the "inside out" instead of from the "outside in," Miller has, over the years, fashioned an integrative psychotherapeutic approach that spotlights teasing out underlying causes of psychological damage, accessing and expanding inner reserves, "befriending" the client's internal life, and undoing/redoing in order to correct for the client's early-on injuries and to extricate him from bonds that have constricted and internal scripts that have obstructed.

With its roots in Clinical Hypnosis, Miller's "Experiential Therapy" is specifically designed to integrate cognitive awareness with sensory perception—thus its emphasis on both what happens inside the mind and the experiencing of things in the body.

Ever respectful, compassionate, heartfelt, generous, and open, Miller —as gifted a writer as he is a clinician—offers both reader and client the "gift of his presence." This magnificent volume is truly a must-read for all clinicians (whether gay or straight) who are committed to helping their clients "unwrap" in order to discover the precious "gifts" that lie within—gifts that had been there all along, just waiting to be found… and opened…

—Martha Stark, MD
Faculty, Harvard Medical School
Author of *Working with Resistance, A Primer on Working with Resistance, and Modes of Therapeutic Action*

UNWRAPPED

Integrative Therapy with Gay Men

... the Gift of Presence

RICK MILLER

ZEIG, TUCKER & THEISEN
Phoenix, Arizona

Unwrapped: Integrative therapy with gay men ... the gift of presence

/ Miller, Rick

p. cm.

Includes bibliographic references
ISBN 978-1-934442-50-0 (alk. paper)
1. Gay men—Mental health. 2. Integrative psychotherapy.
I. Miller, Rick II. Title

Published by

ZEIG, TUCKER & THEISEN
2632 East Thomas Road, Suite 201
Phoenix, AZ 85016

Manufactured in the United States of America

for
Oren Sherman

CONTENTS

Acknowledgements ix

Chapter One: All Is Well ... and It Isn't 1

Chapter Two: Experiential Therapy—a Transformational Approach 13
Script: What Do You Notice in Your Body?
Script: Secure Place

Chapter Three: Growing Up Gay: Then and Now 31
Script: Just Being You
Script: Bypass on the Highway
Script: Rearview Mirror

Chapter Four: The Therapy Relationship: Experience Expansion—Expand Experience 51
Script: Seeing and Knowing You
Script: The Calm After the Storm
Script: Savor Your Impact (for therapists)

Chapter Five: The Myth of the Urban Gay Male 75
Script: Step into the Closet

Chapter Six: Speaking of Sex 87

Chapter Seven: When Sex Is a Problem 111
Script: Healthy Distractions

Chapter Eight: The Shadow of HIV 131
Script: Enhancing Comfort
Script: Rope of Destiny

Chapter Nine: No Room in Heaven: Religion 159
Script: A Strong Foundation

Chapter Ten: Aging Well 175
Script: Inner Circle

Chapter Eleven: Moving Forward: A Generative Life 191
Script: Parade

Bibliography 201

ACKNOWLEDGEMENTS

I was fortunate to be raised in a family with a healthy base. I thank my parents, Samuel and Suzanne Miller, for this and will always appreciate how vital it has been. I wish my father were here to enjoy this milestone.

Stephen and Teri Miller have always lovingly advocated for me. They helped make my becoming a gay adult a positive experience.

Cynthia Mancuso proudly supported me during each evolution of my gay development. (And, she had the best Barbie Doll collection ever.) Throughout this project she taught me the true meaning of resiliency and joy for life. I savor the knowledge that she will enjoy reading this book cover to cover.

My husband, Oren Sherman, has encouraged my success, supported and challenged my intellect, and prompted me to continue growing. His take on people and his use of metaphor have been invaluable. He provided food, warmth and comfort during the several months of compiling this book. He tolerated my being glued to my desk, which took away from time spent together. His pride in me and in this project has been inspirational.

This book has evolved with the mentorship and support of so many people. Over the years, my clients have taught me the most about gay life and how to be a happy man.

Anne Brouse is one of my earliest teachers, and her enthusiasm has greatly influenced me.

Amazing mentors who have inspired me by making learning fun and easy while helping me to appreciate my gifts include, Jeff Zeig,

Claire Frederick, Michael Yapko, and Lise Motherwell. They have all expanded my awareness of the special nature of the therapeutic relationship.

An inexpressible thank you goes to Jeff Zeig. He saw something in me that I had not recognized, and his confidence and generosity steered me toward greater success. As a result, my pride as a gay male professional flourished.

Many thanks to Martha Stark, whose genuine enthusiasm and excitement, which is modeled in her work, has shown me the importance of being my authentic self. The allowance for informality, caring, and humor has only deepened my connection with my clients, while still maintaing respect for the significance of the relationship.

Terry Holzman helped me to appreciate my writing, refine my voice, and actually have fun while doing so.

Derek Polonsky, Dan Short, Martha Stark, and Sue Pinco expressed enthusiasm for my writing, and graciously shared their own literature for my use.

My colleagues and friends, Linda Monahon, Rory Wadlin, Robert Haas, and Ann Webster, have checked in along the way and offered enthusiastic encouragement. A very special thank you goes to Donna Besecker, who provided endless support, read various chapters, and gave me honest feedback.

Ramona Dvorak has always been an inspiring and enthusiastic "mirror," helping me to appreciate my value as psychotherapist.

Decades ago, Bette Jonas Freedson taught me about the importance of using my intuition—a valuable tool that has helped me to be Ericksonian in my work. Years later, we connected again in the Master Class family.

The journey of friendship, via Ann Webster, has brought me to wonderful places with amazing people. Through her, I met two influential people—Susan Dowell, whose love and skill of hypnosis has been instructive and infectious, and Helen Adrienne, who introduced me to Jeff Zeig's Master Class. Helen's warmth continues to welcome me and help me grow, and various friends in the class have now become my chosen family, including Tobi Goldfus, Barbara Birge, Sue Pinco, Hank Griffin, Jeff Munson, Sara Millstein, Harriet Fraad, Lynn Lyons, and Ulrike Jezek.

A specific thank you goes to my "work wife," Tobi Goldfus, who has encouraged me, supported me, laughed with me, and shared numerous travel experiences while we continue to process and grow together. Her confidence in me is constantly reassuring.

Thank you to Sara Blanford for her incredible organizational skills and helping with the bibliography. She made these tasks appear to be so straightforward.

Adelaide, Daisy Mae, and especially Louise (our pups) kept me company for endless hours in my office. They constantly reminded me about the most important lessons in life. Flirting, belly rubs, yummy treats, and leaving the office to go for walks were nonnegotiable. What could be better?

Suzi Tucker, editor and new friend, has exceeded my notions of what a good editor can do. She worked with me gently and intuitively, helping me to shape the book, and reach a higher level. Even more special is her keen ability to see me, appreciate me, and carefully capture my true essence. What a gift for a gay man, given the struggles that I have defined in this book and she has refined. I have unwrapped her presence and will forever savor the impact.

CHAPTER ONE
All Is Well…and It Isn't

Make no mistake about it, themes related to growing up gay are prominent issues when a gay male comes for psychotherapy. Years of self-inhibition have accrued from societal and family messages, even if he hasn't been fully aware of it. The gay client has been editing himself, perhaps for a lifetime. Yes, even now, despite the progress of gay liberation, the gay male client has few people with whom he can be his true self, few environments in which he can feel fully at peace. Most likely, he has chosen to continue living life in a private way, because he has learned that it is safer to edit himself, than risk showing himself. He learned this young, and throughout the years the lesson was likely driven home a thousand times. This has affected every aspect of his existence.

It is essential that we, as therapists, understand this.

Those gay men who make it into psychotherapy are willing to look below the surface and venture deeper, in order to heal the original wound, which is often the source of suffering and inhibition. Bear this in mind as you sit with your new client. Find your way to align with him, and create a connection that feels in synch. The depth of your inquiries and interventions can lead to success in his psychotherapy experience. His ability to acknowledge his pain, coupled with the ability to discover comfort inside his body, will ultimately provide the awareness that all really is well...or can be.

SHAME: THE HALLMARK OF GAY EXISTENCE

Shame stems from internalizing a painful history of negative messages, and then hiding oneself in order to stay safe. Thus, the avoidance of shame becomes the single most powerful driving force in a gay male's life. He himself may not even be aware of it, compartmentalizing it so successfully that he has hidden even from himself.

Gay men are busy being careful. Often, there is an overt reason for concealing themselves from others, yet there is merit in peeling back the layers where more covert reasons can be exposed. The gay man may look "normal" on the outside—successful, well adjusted, happy, and with good friends. On a much subtler level, it may be that he gives just enough—of friendship, affection, and warmth—to be desirable in the eyes of others, while his true self and his deep secrets remain hidden. There is a type of deflection that is carried off automatically with such good skill that many of his close friends and family may not even be aware of it. He may be further away than others realize.

In referencing the experience of a gay man, Alan Downes writes: "If you really knew the whole, unvarnished truth about me, you would know that I am unlovable" (p. xii). Thus, long before being verbal, a gay male censors the truth to make sure he is loved and accepted. This is a reflex, automatic and unconscious.

WHEN THE BODY MEANS BETRAYAL

Growing up, the gay man's body has meant betrayal for him. Perhaps their body carries the message and memory of being effeminate and different from other boys, of not doing well in sports, and then of feeling inadequate as an adult in the face of the images of perfection or the stereotype of the ideal gay male that the media push.

Most gay men have learned to diminish the connection they feel inside. Some are not even aware of having lived this way their entire lives because as a natural response to fear they taught themselves to minimize parts of themselves. They grew up struggling to fit into a world that lived differently from how they felt on the inside. This inconsistency between what is seen and what is felt is not unique to gay men, but it is unique in the way it is experienced by most gay men.

The reality for the majority of gay men is that many years have been spent, or time is still being spent, concealing aspects of their truest selves. Even after being out for years, many gay men continue to hide parts of themselves, without being conscious of doing so.

Fortunately, I have seen resolution of this split in self-identity through a deep experience of inner alignment from trance and the developing awareness that the body can be a friend, an ally. Often, this is a completely new awareness.

UNDOING AND REDOING

The relationship with one's self is a primary factor in successful psychotherapy. We are inviting the client to go inside. We are directly or perhaps indirectly suggesting that there is abundance within the gay male, of which he may not be fully cognizant. This powerful experience that takes place inside his body, with all of his senses, is what I call "undoing and redoing." The client experiences a rejuvenation of his ability to know delight, and two things happen simultaneously: He is undoing the old, internalized way of being. And, he is coming into therapy to work on his presenting issue and getting solutions through the process of experiential work, which in itself is powerful. Yet even more important, he is redoing. On a deeper level he is feeling an internal aliveness through the experiential work that incorporates wholly fresh possibilities. His body is providing for him like never before, because perhaps for the first time he is allowed to be himself, his true self. As this happens, he feels an immense sense of happiness coming from inside his body and he can begin to amplify his happiness, rather than immediately suppress or diminish it.

The internal aliveness I refer to isn't necessarily the reason the client came to therapy, but it becomes primary in the healing that it provides; the fertile ground for solutions to his specified dilemma and for the general potential of future well-being. He begins to feel safe enough to give up his protective shield.

This is especially salient for gay men, as most gay children learn to hide or reject parts of themselves because they have few ways of communicating distress. (Weiss, p. 60) The distress that Weiss refers to and that I will expand upon in Chapter Three, is related to the child's sense that he is different in ways that aren't socially acceptable, and the fact that he has nowhere to go with his feelings.

UNWRAPPED

When we provide psychotherapy to gay men, it is effective to use a cognitive structure that allows our client to appreciate not only that his current circumstances are affecting him in difficult ways, but also that his history might be playing itself out again. What a relief for the client to have a place to sort out these issues, and to have his own psychotherapist advocate to help him understand the reasons why his symptoms are reactivated.

Freedom in experiential therapy occurs when we, as caring clinicians, are providing a special place in which our client can have the unique experience of being the focal point, rather than quietly fading into the background. We offer a chance to create space inside for the real self to emerge whole, instead of melding into a socially expected role with central parts hidden. Here, in our therapy room, the gay man need not be a good boy—quiet and deliberately reserved—something he would have learned as a child that he had to be. He knew at a young age that to be at all flamboyant, or different, or fully honest would be dangerous. Self-editing was an essential tool back then, one that it is not easy to put aside. But in this room, in this moment, we can promote new experiences of life unwrapped!

WHY PSYCHOTHERAPY WITH GAY MEN IS ITS OWN CATEGORY

All too often, gays are lumped together with lesbian, bisexual, transgendered, and queer people. The LGBTQ acronym is a liberal, politically correct way of referring to the group at-large, and a quick succinct way to be inclusive. However, each group has issues of its own, different from the others, and based on their own history gay men have a particular cluster of issues. The expectations that come from the gay community and from society in general, also create certain pressures. The details and uniqueness of these issues are spelled out in this book. Reading this book will give you access to a host of insider tips, both from the perspective of a gay male, and from a psychotherapist with 30 years of experience in working with gay men.

This book focuses on the most relevant global issues that affect gay men and provides well-rounded discussions on how to cope with them. Customized experiential scripts, theoretical perspectives, and case examples will help guide your therapeutic approach. You will gain an in-depth understanding about the uniqueness of the gay male world, something that should be compulsory for all providers. You will also be able to be bolder in addressing specific topics in psychotherapy with your gay male clients that may be difficult, and will enjoy using your creativity and intuition to make your work more personal and energizing. Whether you are working with one gay man among dozens of heterosexual clients, working with many gay men, or are simply gaining a knowledge base for yourself, this book offers an important aspect of education: readiness and preparedness. After all, sooner rather than later a gay man will be entering your office, and though his presenting issue may take any number of forms, being a gay man will be part of his constellation.

Awareness of what it means to be a gay man has grown exponentially. Societal acceptance, as reflected by more positive portrayal of gay men in the media, support for gay youth and their families, and an increase in the number of states allowing gay marriage (and in countries throughout the world), marks progress for gay men. Internal wounds may be somewhat alleviated by these changes and communities that once had absolutely no awareness of what it means to be gay, now have access to information. All of this creates a positive ripple effect for gay males of this generation. Early awareness comes sooner, families are more able to understand what it means, and the internal battle of self-acceptance is often less punitive than it has been for generations past.

Despite this, many gay men have not had the good fortune to grow up in an accepting atmosphere, and continue to experience conflict, internally and externally. Of course, pain is not unique to gay men. However, the specific reasons that they experience pain, and the ways in which they deal (or do not deal) with it are unique. The history and personal development of gay males is different than it is for everyone else, including other minorities, who at least have the support of their families and communities, since they are so often part of the same minority.

The sense of alienation that is experienced is strikingly similar among gay men. My own experience of growing up gay, and my current identity questions and self-esteem issues are all remarkably resonant with my gay male clients. The combination of gender expectations and self-introjections from society impose a heavy load to be carried—even now.

The fact that a man has come out of the closet doesn't mean the journey is over. Often, the undertones of sadness linger for a very long time. The power of experiential work with gay men lies in part in providing an opportunity for these men to lovingly and affirmatively come back to the body as a safe place, to be present with everything as it is, and to move into the future in an open way.

Even though foliage on a tree may appear intact, the root system is the most important part of vitality and longevity. It is the part that cannot be seen, because it is underground. The challenge of psychotherapy with gay males is to appreciate the causes of damage to the root system and to know the best ways of helping to make repairs. It is never too late to make change. Providing a healthy environment ensures an essential growing space in which to expand and flourish.

The scripts that are included in this book come directly from my clinical practice with gay men. They are inspired by the work I do and the experience I have had, both as a professional and a gay man. While they may be used in other settings, these scripts are tailored to meet the milestones, concerns, and histories of gay male clients.

This book will help you become more comfortable and bolster your confidence in working with gay men, as you come to appreciate specific issues relevant to them. And, you will discover ways to address those issues. It is always important that we as therapists be informed about the various backgrounds of the people with which we work. We always want to have a base of awareness that will allow us to work effectively and confidently with our clients.

In addition, it is refreshing to be stimulated and reminded about things that we already know. Thus, this book will enhance work beyond specific treatment with gay men.

I'M HOOKED

Following my first Master Class in Ericksonian hypnosis, a four-day experiential course led by Dr. Jeffrey K. Zeig, I was skeptical about this new world into which I had stumbled. In the taxi back to the airport, I wasn't certain that this work was suitable for me, since it was expressive in ways that my contained self wasn't accustomed. Within a couple of days of returning back to work, I realized something inside of me had shifted. At the time, it was difficult to describe and impossible to ignore. I emailed Jeff Zeig with the message, "I fell into the whole. I'm hooked."

The power of experiential work made me feel different as a gay male, and as a clinician. It took me longer to appreciate this than it did my clients, perhaps because I felt I had more at stake. Professionally, I had an entirely new learning set on which to embark, and after 25 years of clinical practice, this was overwhelming. But it was clear and it remains clear that experiential work is pivotal. The power comes from integrating cognitive awareness and sensory awareness—feeling it, really feeling it—and getting it, with an emphasis on resourcefulness. Resourcefulness instead of pathology was something new for me.

THE EXPERIENTIAL REALM

In the last several years I have expanded my focus in my clinical approach to include much more experiential work. I have found that it is even more beneficial for patients to experience something, to feel it, rather than to just hear it. This layer includes all sensory experiences, such as physical feeling, emotional sensation and memory, whether sound, smell, taste, or visual image. Any and all of these may serve as powerful reminders in piecing a puzzle together. These sensory experiences, which are not just cognitively processed, but experienced on a multitude of levels, provide a depth that awakens internal power, which can be life altering for a gay male. Perhaps he experiences this strength from doing experiential work for the first time in his life, because like many gay men, he had never learned to befriend his body.

In the course of growing up, we all experience societal pressure to *be* certain ways, and to *not be* other ways. As gay men, our heads become filled with notions of what it means to be a boy (Hedges, p. 15), and there is a momentous tragedy of human existence when the spontaneity and creative sensuous expressions of early childhood become socially bound, and channeled in our personalities. (Hedges, p. 12)

As clinicians, we are empowering patients to feel good about themselves. And if you are a male clinician, you might even be the first male in your client's life who can see him as possessing strength. To be seen in this way is something for which all gay males wish. Again, it is true that all of us likely wish for this experience. Still, for gay men, the experience is so often completely out of reach that a therapist's positive view of the client can be life changing, and mark a new beginning.

In earlier times, therapy was relegated to contact with the client's past and digging up painful, unpleasant materials in order to appreciate what caused the damage. In fact, patients have a host of positive memories that can be accessed and utilized as resources. (Frederick, 1999) It is refreshing for a gay male to have a positive focus in his treatment, since so much of his life has been secretive or viewed, even by him, as pathology-based.

Happiness is an experiential reality. (Zeig, 2006) Therapy is the reassociation of an internal life, and this can happen quickly and easily. (Zeig, 2006) It is always exciting to do experiential work with clients who feel stuck and to see the difference, sometimes instantaneously. (Pinco, 2008) Learning from the inside out (Zeig, 2006) is what makes experiential work successful. Gay men are so often busy living from the outside in!

ALEX:

After years of therapy Alex asked to try experiential work to see whether it would help him with his stress and physical discomfort.

Alex is a 38-year-old gay male who has considerable anxiety and agitation about daily life events and often worries that they will precipitate another manic episode. He presents with tightness and tension in his entire body, especially in his face as he clenches his jaws, and_around his eyes, which appear strained. (I sometimes feel myself clenching my jaws too, picking up on his stress.) My hope is that experiential work will give him the opportunity to learn to appreciate his own strength and stability from the inside, and to come to trust the power of his own resources.

THE PROCESS

To start, I simply have Alex relax fully in his body, soften the muscles around his face and neck, appreciate how the softness feels and how it allows him to breathe deeply and comfortably.

I watch his face soften and direct his awareness to how his facial muscles are relaxing. I now see him in a new way, a way that shows me what he truly looks like without the fearful tightness from head to toe. His physical attributes become stronger and his attractiveness shines in ways that it previously had not.

During the trance state, I ask him to describe what it is that he is aware of, and he asks himself out loud, "Why is it so hard to remember that I have the power to become relaxed inside? I forget I have the power to relax. I see myself inside a cage and I want to get myself out. I am not the awful person I felt for so long. I am deserving. I am important." He holds his head up high in this moment. "I cannot and will not give up trying to make things better for myself. I can rise above negativity!"

When he opens his eyes, he warmly looks at me smiling and says, "This was better than a benzo!"

"YOU CAN"

As a gay man, I am very comfortable being myself and I use this comfort in sessions, which serves as a model for gay male clients. With this stance, I indirectly imply, "I am confident in myself, and you can be too." This goes a long way in helping them to infer that they might find comfort as well.

Patients come to therapy for experiences, not necessarily for understandings. (Zeig, 2006) Each time we provide a positive experience for the client, particularly early on in his treatment, he will be encouraged to bond, and also to trust both the relationship and the belief that we have in him.

"You can" is what my mentor, Jeff Zeig, has taught me. This deep lesson is carried on multiple levels. In fact, "you can" has become the underpinning of my own clinical work. Often clients are taken by surprise. Having grown up feeling rejected or disconnected, this message seems incongruent. The power of it evokes a sense of strength and possibility that can be brand new, no matter one's chronological age. Feeling inadequate is suddenly undone and the opposite feeling is redone in an instant.

I too have felt the power of this experience during work with therapists, supervisors, and mentors, whose encouragement fills me with strength and possibility. Whether it is a direct "you can," or it is implied, I marvel at the wonderful feeling of being seen, supported, and encouraged.

Imaginal processes assume the feel of real memories and offer a profound and reparative connection to those parts of the self that have been disowned. This process generates a nurturing attachment to a loving, caretaking, and nurturing self that can repair the damage done in earlier times. These experiences overlay old traumatic memories. When clients are able to do this, with the support of a connected therapist, they are able to make dramatic shifts in their relationship to themselves and to others. (Pinco, 2008)

The possibility of this shift is so essential when working with gay men. The outcome of these experiences makes ongoing work with clients much more powerful. The broader view of metaphor, to be expanded, enhanced, and enriched, creates the space for new experiences, reactions, and meaning systems. (Pinco, 2008) Borrowing an idea from Helen Adrienne's work and applying it to the current topic: When you can accept being gay—what it means, and no longer means—you then deepen mind/body awareness. There is an implicit respect for the indisputable unity of mind and body. (Adrienne, 2011)

In doing experiential work, a gay male client achieves treatment goals, while also discovering a bridge to his past and future. The difficult experiences he had in the past loses their potency in the present, as he is able to have internal focus, reliance on his entire self (without automatic compartmentalization), expansion of internal resources, exposure of his vulnerabilities, and acceptance by you, the therapist. The bridge is crossed with a freedom of being his true self. He is able to discard his protective shield, stops editing, and sheds his fears of rejection. Experiential work proves its merit, so that his future life can be more fulfilling. Of course, we must all be warned: Growth is not a straight line! (Adrienne, 2011, p 161)

The experiential work I am trained in is clinical hypnosis. Many of my references throughout this book will be about hypnosis, and the language may be hypnosis language. However, you can choose your own modality of experiential work that best fits your style. You can adapt the scripts that I provide in any way that fits. My focus throughout is working with gay men. An experiential approach is the primary motive, but without an understanding of the covert dilemmas in which gay men are caught, no approach will have real resonance.

CHAPTER TWO

Experiential Therapy—A Transformational Approach

WHAT THE CLIENT MAY EXPERIENCE AS EXPERIENTIAL WORK

Most of our clients have already tried to modify their lives. When they contact us it is in part because they feel unable to reach their potential on their own. The respect you show for a client's openness to guidance is a relief to him. It's a great way to start treatment. Even if it's someone else who insists that the person come for treatment, it is he, the client, who makes the choice to enter the office. And we know that if he has made it this far, there is a good chance he will do the work needed in psychotherapy to make real change.

Keep in mind though, that gay male clients who are willing to do experiential work may be reticent about doing something different from traditional therapy. Remember their history. Trying something unusual, especially with eyes closed (assuming he is even willing), may evoke trust issues that are still on the table. Experiential work can be a scary, unfamiliar territory. Some clients are direct about their uncertainty, while others imply it in their tone or body posture. Bringing this out into the open may be all that the client needs in order to proceed. Without the pressures of perfection, and with the therapist's awareness (and acceptance) of a client's diffidence, the goals of the experience become more realistic.

If we feel comfortable suggesting that a client try experiential work and are reassuring about its safety while demonstrating confidence, then we set an encouraging tone. This level of intervention immediately and indirectly establishes a "you can" moment. And just saying yes to this opportunity may allow your client to discover a new or revived sense of internal confidence.

Clients with anxiety or trauma histories may initially be leery of experiential work. It is best to focus on safety and control without pushing them beyond their comfort zone. Before starting, a straightforward explanation frames expectations. Most clients are familiar with some kind of breathing exercises or meditation, or even yoga, and clarifying the common ground with these experiential approaches can put the mind at ease.

People with painful histories may assume they don't have the ability to do or experience anything positive. They don't yet recognize internal resources. Simply sharing stories about other clients who felt the same way initially but were able to develop comfort in doing hypnosis can make all the difference.

INTERNAL RESOURCES

Experiential work emphasizes internal resources. This may be disconcerting for a client who isn't aware of how much strength he already possesses. My job as an experiential therapist is to help him discover, expand, and trust his resources.

Therapy that centers on pathology tends to reinforce diagnosis. The trouble with this is that clients sometimes build their entire self-view on years of diagnosis. That image becomes part of the problem.

But in your therapy room, with you as his guide, your client has the opportunity to experience himself in an important new way—as inherently resourced, with strengths not yet plumbed. For clients who have been in years of therapy, the sense of moving forward is refreshing. Many clients don't want to go back to rehash what their parents did to them; they want to focus on the issue at hand.

From natural endowments—talents, intelligence, and abilities—to the training, education and success acquired in life, our clients' resources are just waiting to be acknowledged and put to further use. (Frederick, 1999) People are often dissociated from their own resources and need help locating and recognizing them.

The goal of experiential work is to help the client experience and enhance the true definition of self. Cognitive, conscious, and logical thought can dampen or modulate our client's emotions, but it will not help change the underlying structures that give rise to the emotions or facilitate healing. An experience of change in therapy is something that can be extrapolated into the world. As one client put it, "I am usually living in two states: zombie and fragile. But hypnosis woke me up! I have a third state, which is alive and able to take care of myself."

Jeff Zeig puts it this way: "You do not learn to ride bicycle in your left hemisphere, you learn to ride a bicycle in your body. You try and you fall and you try again. After a while, you are suddenly doing it. Your body learns and you have got it!" (Zeig, 2006, p. 31)

Experiential work fosters a deeper, richer, and more powerful therapy experience, especially when, as a matter of survival, clients have not in the past accessed the full spectrum of the self. If we ask a client to recall something that occurred when he was 6 years old, he may be able to offer a report and even re-experience some of the sensations from that time.

However, if we ask the same question and then invite him to notice what is happening inside his body as he remembers the event from long ago, he will likely have greater access to the breadth and depth of memory. Additional layers may come into awareness: what he was wearing, the sounds, the smells, and quality of light. Even with eyes open the client becomes absorbed in the memory in its broad dimension, and dissociated from the present in a healthy way.

In a state of trance, direct or indirect, clients have the potential to establish new associations, new awareness, and new skills, as well as the ability to connect to personal resources. (Yapko, 2012) Asking the client to really notice what it is that he is experiencing inside his body, how his body is communicating to him, and what his body has to say, are invitations for him to experience himself more fully than he may be used to. This is important because gay male clients need to have experiences in which the body provides different information than what was received in the past—information that is positive, resourced, and forward-looking.

The following demonstrates how you might shape an invitation to clients to go inside.

Script: What Do You Notice in Your Body? (Body Awareness)

Really, really pay attention.

Overlooking internal awareness is common for gay men. Having permission to access an awareness that has long been hidden generates opportunities for growth that come from within, rather than from the therapist. Often, we are trained to be thinking cognitively rather than to gain full access to the depth of information that is available to use.

With these few sentences, either in conversation or in a state of trance, a new space can open up:

> *You can appreciate what it is that is happening inside of you. You may not be aware that within yourself, your own body, there are ways that you can listen for what you may not know, and things that you would like to know. Just notice thoughts that you are having in this moment. Excellent.* [Adding encouragement throughout scripts is important, as clients generally respond well to recognition and affirmation.] *Notice images that come to you in this moment, like pictures in your mind. You might even notice emotions that you feel or physical sensations inside of your body. Good. Really pay attention to what it is that comes to you. Just be open to whatever these images, thoughts, and sensations are, and it doesn't even matter whether you can make sense of what all this means, we will discuss it in a few moments.*

This exercise is always powerful, particularly with clients who are heavily cognitive. The simple encouragement can begin to guide the client toward the resources needed to empower him in finding solutions on his own.

Experiential work often provides such a sense of relief that clients feel it immediately. Restrictive norms can be transformed in moments. Providing a setting in which to let go, to even have some fun, may mark the beginning of positive change in our clients' lives.

ERICKSONIAN WORK

The Ericksonian therapy lens is essential to the success of my experiential work. Milton Erickson's approach was to emphasize natural abilities within each client. The paradigm holds that nothing needs to be added from the outside; all the answers exist within, even if the client is not aware of it. Erickson's model was based on elicitation, awakening and stimulating dormant resources, and the expectancy of success. (Frederick, 1999; O'Hanlon, 1989) This is pretty powerful, especially for gay men, who are used to minimizing their own resources, and relying on the approval of others.

The job of the therapist is to re-contextualize existing resources to stimulate the dormant possibilities within the client. (Zeig, 2006) Erickson preferred an indirect approach that allowed people to make their own meanings. (Frederick, 1999; O'Hanlon, 1989) It is more evocative, and thus effective, for the client to make his own meaning from what we say or what he experiences. Sometimes I think that Erickson created this approach specifically to help gay men come into their own.

Erickson's success with his patients was a function of his ability to discern their uniqueness and to use it as a pathway to form successful therapeutic alliances, build expectations, and tap into the patient's resources. This is key to the "you can" approach that he advocated.

Erickson did not promote insight as the means of precipitating change. This is significant. Many theoretical orientations are mostly insight-oriented. They help a client to understand things but don't provide the simultaneous experience of success, in other words, without the experiential opportunity for that insight to be anchored in the body.

From an Ericksonian view, the therapist doesn't even need to know the cause of the client's symptoms in order to resolve them. Instead, the therapist can encourage a more evocative focus. This is another profound aspect for gay men who are often so good at analysis, but not as skilled at allowing their own sense of freedom and creativity to take the lead. Analysis is the safest place for people who have been taught implicitly and explicitly that their intuition leads to negative consequences. Here again, we provide the space to undo and redo some basic instincts.

It may not even be so urgent to take a formal history in the first few sessions. It is more important to establish rapport, to provide a meaningful experience, and to emphasize resourcefulness so that clients appreciate what therapy offers. The history will come out over time.

For professionals steeped in a traditional psychotherapy background there are challenges, but the clients' responses will convince you. It's not theoretical—it's experiential!

BEING HYPNOTIC VERSUS DOING HYPNOSIS

One can be hypnotic without doing hypnosis. To Erickson, hypnosis wasn't just a trance state with a client, it was a context for interpersonal communication and process. (Zeig, 2006)

Being aware of yourself and how you communicate, and recognizing that the suggestions you provide are an inevitable part of this interpersonal mix, are essential Ericksonian principals. (Yapko, 2012; Zeig, 2006) One's vocabulary is more than words. A variety of physical and auditory considerations is available: for example, a different tone of voice to emphasize an important point or leaning forward to underscore the desire to really hear the client, or a quick smile to indicate encouragement or a deep breath to demonstrate relaxation.

Your creativity and confidence will grow as you gather affirmative experiences from clients. Experiential therapy is reciprocal! Your clients don't want you to be a blank slate, they want you to be connected and engaging. This position not only says something about you, it implicitly says something about your interaction with them.

The creative moment in experiential work is where the magic happens. The most effective treatment emerges through customizing sessions for each client rather than using verbatim scripts or protocols. Customization and attunement begins with the first encounter. Then, creativity flows in a natural way that feels organic. As we allow ourselves to let go—of rigidity, of fear, of our own critical voices—we become less concerned with the perfect intervention, as we simultaneously become more attuned to our clients' needs. Becoming exquisitely aware of those needs, we open ourselves to incorporating them (utilization) into the specific interventions. This deepens a client's experience. Being seen and understood will invoke delight in him. The value of this experience will come to life for him inside your office, and he will bring this to other places in his life.

RYAN:

Ryan is a 42-year-old gay man with moderate anxiety. He links his current struggles to his childhood, and to his alcoholic father. His father, who often called him a bozo, died when Ryan was a young boy. Ryan internalized the harsh messages from his father and others, and his feelings of shame and alienation.

Ryan is excited to try hypnosis to gain control of his current stress and he takes to it immediately. He easily goes into a very relaxed place. A basic relaxation can really surprise a client, as a feeling of comfort accompanied by the ability to access long dormant inner qualities happens so quickly. It is immediately beneficial for Ryan to recognize that he possesses the ability to feel a sense of internal calm. I use the Secure Space script (provided later in this chapter) with him.

Ryan arrives the following week saying, "It was really, really great for me to go inside like that, and I have never before had the experience of feeling so good inside of myself."

***

This is a clear example of the indirect nature of Ericksonian work. In a direct way, Ryan was able to experience true relaxation. Indirectly, he became aware that all by himself, he had both the capacity to achieve a state of feeling good and the ability to recognize that feeling. I knew that I would use this strength in future hypnosis sessions with issues pertaining to being gay and their connection to his anxiety.

***

While doing hypnosis in a subsequent session, Ryan tearfully recalls having decided as a child, "I was always going to be a good boy and work hard to make everything work. Even though I am 42, I have never put these pieces together before today. I often feel guilty, and I feel guilty for even saying that I feel guilty."

"I always went along with what was around me. That is how I functioned. I never said what I wanted. It is the past and it has been a habit, but my new place is stronger. There are no expectations." Then, he spontaneously said to himself, "Grow up."

Ryan talks about being gay and always having to be careful. "I always protect myself by staying away from others." I decide it would be most effective to reframe aloneness and ask him to remember a time when he was alone and it felt okay.

He describes being a kid after school: "After school, I would walk to the trails in the woods near our house, sit on a stump and overlook the town. I would just sit and feel quite content. It brought me comfort, being and sitting there. Then I would walk home. It was my own private little magical place"

While he is in trance, I elaborate on the significance for him of having his private place just for himself, and I speak to him about being happy. I emphasize that he, all by himself, knew what he needed and wanted, understanding exactly how to care for himself in all the right ways. In asking him to connect to that younger kid, I was indirectly suggesting that his vulnerabilities were no longer going to be a deterrent for him and that being gay would no longer hold him back. This turns out to be a good choice. He describes a deep inner understanding: "I feel relieved, now I see the big picture."

This is not an opportunity that I am willing to miss out on, so using the "big picture" metaphor I have him imagine he is holding a photo album. He responds, "I see pictures of me and my old dog with family and many friends surrounding me. I look at them and see things I want: freedom, more time, balance, more satisfying relationships."

I tell him that he can imagine picking up another photo album that shows more big pictures and he continues, "I see family pictures of me and my partner loving life, enjoying a life filled with friends, travel, and creative endeavors."

Then he adds something that comes from deep inside these images, an insight that could only come from him. "I just had a revelation about my life. I always say that I am lonely when, in fact, I am not. Sometimes, I am just stressed. Reaching out for someone to verify me is an old behavior and I don't really need it anymore. My new puzzle is put together."

Typically, when Ryan comes out of a session, I see a powerful energy and sparkle in him that he says feels every time. This is common for people who enjoy doing experiential work.

A LITTLE MORE ABOUT HYPNOSIS

People are mystified and intrigued by the concept of hypnosis, and many are frightened by what they think could happen.("Will you make me cluck like a chicken?") I explain that hypnosis is actually a gentle, relaxing process that clients will most likely enjoy and remember. Further, I let them know that through it they will be able to use their own resources to work on their problems. With my guidance, hypnosis becomes a tool for them to reclaim—or claim for the first time—their freedom.

The various experiential approaches available are much more similar than dissimilar. (Brown, 2010; Yapko, 2012) Hypnosis incorporates elements of self-focus and relaxation. The therapist begins with an induction. This deepening process steers the client away from external experience toward his inner experience: what he hears, notices, thinks or feels. Then, through imagination, or imagery or shifts in attention, the client has the ability to experience things quite differently than he usually does. There is an element of expansion that takes place—an expansion of resourcefulness, awareness, comfort or strength. Thus, the client's innate abilities are quickly within his reach, and with them solutions and coping mechanisms begin to come alive.

In the majority of hypnotic interactions, clients appear to be sitting passively or merely absorbing the suggestions of the clinician. In reality, clients are actively participating in the process and searching for the relevance of suggestions, particularly when the suggestions hold the potential of helping them solve personal distress. (Yapko, 2012)

When I do hypnosis with my clients I think of experiential work as a series of brief descriptive scenes that focus on one moment and are strategic in nature. Each session is a scene that has its own rhythm and tone. Each vignette has a purpose, such as meeting my client's goals, or even the goals that I set during a particular session. No matter how often I do hypnosis with the same client, the vignette is different each time.

KARL:

Karl wants to be seen immediately. He comes to my office depressed and isolated following a tough breakup with his boyfriend. He feels suicidal.

As soon as I meet him I realize I don't need to worry about his suicidal thoughts. It is clear to me that he has a resourceful, receptive part of himself that he has discredited.

We do hypnosis in the first session. In hypnosis, he instantly relaxes. His body and face appear less strained, and while his breathing becomes steadier and deeper, I watch him settle into his comfort.

In this session he has an important realization, an expansion of his normal understanding: "I have been so busy responding to the emotional reactions of others so sensitively, that I have allowed them to negatively affect me. I have choices."

Around the third session of hypnosis, and with a growing trust between us, Karl identifies a long-hidden part of himself. It is another powerful revelation. "There is a proud part. And that part has gotten me where I am now in my life. I have had many accomplishments."

I ask him if this newly discovered part of him could speak to the less confident, nonbelieving part of him. The proud part says, "It is very important for you to listen to me. I am the part that is strong. I am here, I have been with you, and you may have forgotten that I am here, but I haven't left. It makes me sad that you forget I am here, yet I am happy because I have been able to make it very far in my life."

Karl then talks about seeing an image of himself in his 20s. "I am newly out and it feels fresh and exciting. I realize that my current lonely feelings are a result of the breakup. A breakup is not the same as suicidality. I was more profoundly depressed back then, and I am not feeling that way now." Next, he has a visual image of the proud part and the less secure part melding together. He nearly bellows, "I have arrived!"

How amazing to witness his transformation. He can now fully inhabit his body and his life. The vulnerable meek man who had walked into my office has become strong and confident. His past has been acknowledged and his present unwrapped!

***

Through hypnosis he experienced a shift that was different than his usual state of consciousness. As a result, he was able to access imagery, fantasy, and emotion, and decrease defensiveness and increase receptiveness. I didn't have to direct or lead him; he took himself where he needed to go.

***

BRAD:

Brad is a 47-year-old gay man who has had depression for years and has been in and out of long-term therapy. Though he complains of being depressed, I do not see him as depressed. He is animated and doesn't show any of the classic symptoms of major depression. It seems that years ago he was told he was depressed and the label stuck.

One day Brad begins, "If I hadn't been depressed my entire life..." and I wonder aloud how that definition has tainted his frame of self-reference. He agrees to do hypnosis and explore what depression means.

"I feel guilty and bad. I monitor other people's behavior carefully. My behavior as a boy was not okay, so I learned to monitor it closely so I didn't seem gay or weak. It's exhausting."

I ask him if the adult part of him could offer the child part of him any help.

"The adult part of me gives little faggy me more protection and love, so I don't need to edit, censor, or be hypervigilant anymore. However, little faggy me is still cautious about being out. This is how I have lived—dead, low energy, resentful that I am here. I am better than this. I deserve more than this. My posture is closed, hunched, head down, strained. I can't tolerate it. I could be doing so much more." My intrinsic capabilities allow me to move forward. I can choose to leave the past behind. I feel like I am moving toward my creative work now."

The following week, Brad reports he felt a glimpse of what he could have more of: "A core that I have only felt vaguely, now I feel more of, plus a sense that I will get more of what I need in this place." Although long-term talk therapy would eventually bring him to these realizations, experiential work brings him here quickly, on his own, and in a felt sense.

Brad is an artist. During his hypnosis, we explore weaving as a metaphor for his being able to restructure the threads inside of him and recognize that he will not unravel in the process. He can use his own inner raw materials and put them together to be more cohesive. This metaphor is meaningful for him.

Script: Secure Place

The Secure Space script is a great start so clients can appreciate that safety is central to our work together. When people try this for the first time they are usually pleasantly surprised. Many clients enjoy the tone of my voice and comment that it is reassuring. Learning to use one's voice effectively is a helpful tool. Sometimes the most powerful experience is for our clients to realize that they have the capacity to relax within. In the case of gay men, who have learned that the body is dangerous and their innate abilities cannot be trusted, this release may be extremely profound. Subsequent sessions can be paced to add more experience, little by little.

The Secure Space script (and its variations) is used in several experiential modalities. The purpose is to use the metaphor of safety to remind clients that they have the resources to create and to maintain a sense of security by themselves.

Following a basic induction, or my body awareness exercise (earlier in the chapter), the script may be used and adapted according to the needs of the client.

> *And now that you are feeling relaxed, you appreciate how good it feels to be in this place inside. Even if it feels like a long time since you have been in this place, you can appreciate a*

time in the past, either recently, or even a long time ago, when you felt this way.

Perhaps you can remember being in a place in nature, a place on vacation, or even a really comfortable place inside your home. [Have them explore this in-depth, as this is the source of the power of the exercise.] If nothing comes to you, you can even use this moment here with me, as your own special place.

Clients may be impressed by their capacity to enjoy the experience using their own abilities, and yours as well. We can remind them that in doing this work they have accessed their own resources. I try not to get too caught up in providing a detailed cognition of what they will experience, since just doing it is the best way to appreciate its power.

Keep in mind that for gay men, the issue of trust is always front and center. The gay male client needs to be sure he can trust you, and given his history of having to hide from others in order to feel safe and to be accepted, this is understandable. It isn't necessary (or persuasive) to go overboard explaining that you are comfortable with a client who is gay; it is most effective to simply show it, to actually be comfortable. Mutual respect will develop quickly and the power of the work will emerge once the container of trust is established.

THERAPEUTIC REWARDS

If we feel comfortable being creative and using our intuition to guide us while leading experiential work, we will be rewarded with a natural collaboration with our clients. By attuning to their ways of expressing themselves, we can pluck resonant words, images, and sensations that can be used during sessions.

Over the years I have come to trust my intuition in sessions. I don't always know why I am seeing or imagining things as I sit with my clients, but I do know that the co-creation of the moment is informing me. I have learned to incorporate what comes to me into hypnosis in my own way. When an image emerges, I share it, saying something like, "You can imagine seeing ...", or, "And though I am not exactly sure why this is coming to me in this moment, I am sure that you will experience the meaning that is just right for you."

Even a client's resistance can be enlisted. Of course it is difficult when we

encounter resistance, particularly when we are somewhat new to this kind of work. We still feel self-conscious about potential outcomes. However, as you develop comfort with incorporating clients' resistance into the experiential session—it is a part of his vocabulary, after all—you can soften your expectation, and the tone of the session will probably shift. The more you engage creatively, the easier it becomes, and the more secure you become in the process.

THE PARALLEL PROCESS THAT COMES AS A SURPRISE

Psst, to the therapist...you may notice that when I suggest that you work on using your creativity, there may be a part of you inside that tenses up or goes limp. I may be asking you to stretch yourself in ways in which you are not accustomed.

This is similar to what a gay man feels as you invite him into experiential work. Bound by traditions, if you will, of family norms or societal expectations, he has a history of molding himself in a certain way, sometimes far from who he really is. He may be so far from it, in fact, that he doesn't even know who he really is yet. When he is able to find a way to let himself go just a bit more to be less constricted, he feels better. You can help him do this. By the same token, as you deepen your comfort to be more creative and less constricted with your clients, you will feel better too—freer and invigorated.

The best way you can teach letting go is by experiencing it yourself and modeling it. A rigid therapist is not going to be able to offer this dimension of healing—the part that tells him that it is safe to color outside the lines; that he can trust himself. Just as I ask my clients to appreciate what they are feeling inside their body and to really pay attention to this, I ask you to do that too.

Instead of editing, allow what comes to you to be something that you treasure and utilize in a positive way. It really makes a difference in your clinical work. This is essential when working with gay men. More and more, you will be free and enjoy the results. He will learn from you and be able to do the same.

As therapists, we must have a breadth of knowledge regarding the social and historical context of the people with whom we work. Growing up as a gay male has its own cluster of particularities. Whether or not you are a gay man, if you are going to treat this population you need to be comfortable and compassionate regarding the common backgrounds of most gay men– as well as sharp and perceptive when it comes to the varied effects that may show up in therapy. Knowledge of and ease with experiential approaches is an especially important addition to therapy with gay men, as it invites an understanding of new possibilities that goes beyond the intellect. Often, a sense of immediate relief, release, and rejuvenation takes root in the session and the client is able to easily hold this opening as he exits the room and reenters his life.

YOU GO FIRST

Creating change in therapy comes from movement. The more you are able to let go, the more your client will benefit. He will find himself able to try things he has never tried before, and will enjoy the success. You go first.

Tips for Letting Go

Allow your sensory experiences to flourish. Not only will you be nourished, you will also have wonderful experiences to incorporate into your work.

- Keep alert for images, stories, and metaphors that pop up in your daily life. Gather them and bring them in to your therapy office—these are things from which to draw. You must be quick and improvisational when working experientially. There is no wasted knowledge!

- Stay open. And make sure you communicate this through your posture, the timbre of your voice, and the expressions that move across your face. What you actually say will be more resonate.
- Remember, humor is a powerful tool, especially with gay men. Learn to effectively use humor during a session, keeping the right balance of lightness and seriousness.
- Take some risks in your work with clients. You are educated, experienced, and skilled. Creativity and intuition may prove to be the ingredients that enliven your experience of the work. Gay men will especially benefit from your willingness to explore this.

CHAPTER THREE

Growing Up Gay: Then and Now

At 8 years old, Simon was already aware of his loneliness, isolation, and sadness. One day, as he was slowly making his way to school, he noticed a weed growing up through the sidewalk. In that moment, Simon knew something important, something absolutely life altering—that he was going to be okay.

***

Long before you know you are gay, before you understand what it is, you know you are different from others. Somehow, being a boy in the way that people expect you to be just doesn't feel quite right. You don't talk about it; maybe it's not even in your consciousness yet, but the feeling is there. It's uncomfortable, confusing, isolating, and sometimes frightening. And even though your parents already may know, you hope to god they don't. You pray that no one sees, and you spend a lot of excruciating effort hiding this secret that you cannot even exactly name yet.

I call this process, common to almost all gay men, "hiding in." From a very early age, this boy feels that he must create a meticulous protective shield, and as time goes by, the shield becomes nearly impenetrable. Most gay men bring this shield with them into adulthood.

For the gay child, the tension between the internal world and external world is hard to bear. Internally, what has to be kept secret is a constant source of shame. Externally, he knows well the expectations of others and he becomes very good at navigating them. He doesn't have the same interests as other boys, and finds that he is drawn to toys and games that are considered feminine. No matter where he looks, the reflection that comes back tells him that his interests are not okay, not normal.

He learns that it is risky to openly demonstrate interests that lie outside of typical male behavior (Weiss, 2005), and so hiding in becomes a life focus that is fraught with fear and anxiety. He must keep parts of himself secret at all costs. As a result, a false self emerges in order that he might have connections with others. (Cadwell, 2009)

The opposite of hiding in is, of course, coming out, something most young boys, especially in the past, wouldn't feel safe to do. It wasn't safe, and to a great extent still isn't. Thus, the shield, rather than being made of metal, is made of other, more invisible materials: the need to stay private, the instinct to be reserved, the avoidance of free expression, and the general suppression of self.

Such themes, which stem from childhood, tend to be part of the narrative into adulthood. But it is never too late to intervene, no matter how late. Experiential work offers a unique opportunity to help the client put down his shield, while feeling spacious and safe, so that hiding in is no longer a reflex. Through this work, clients can experience what Simon experienced all those years ago: that it is possible to blossom, no matter the environment in which one grows up.

Remember, this approach is highly collaborative. Gay or straight, you need to honestly ask yourself a few questions before moving forward.

Orienting Questions

- Are you willing to encourage your client to explore painful parts of his history when necessary? Will you be able to stay with it even when he resists, or is scared?

- Can you abide hearing how he was bullied or degraded, while maintaining a caring but respectful stance with him?
- Can you maintain the focus on a positive resolution for him without demonizing those who tormented him?
- Can you tolerate hearing details about his flamboyancy during childhood, especially if it is unusual within the scope of your own experiences, or goes against the way that you were raised? Can you maintain your care no matter what?

PLANTING THE SEEDS OF FREEDOM

It is important to establish a stance of freedom as you work with gay men. He should feel that your connection is specifically to him, that you really see him and hear him. This is essential for him to feel safe, and it will go far in helping him to feel that the protective shield is not necessary as he sits with you. In creating an open environment, the course of therapy is an evolutionary process. The timing of experiential work, for instance, will depend on the client. Should a history be taken now or later? Do you need to delve deeply, or has he already been in so much therapy before, that a lighter touch is now needed? You are guiding clients toward a more alive, and abundant present. Being generic or rigid would be antithetical to what you want to model.

Being cognizant of a historical perspective is important: his freedom has inevitably been curtailed as he tried to fit in; by squelching his creativity, his joy and his love, he has likely built up a store of regret; and there may be numerous leftover pieces that continue to play out in subtle ways as an adult. These are all central themes in his life. And, they will be central themes in your therapy.

Hypnosis, or any kind of experiential work, offers a way to plant new seeds. Through it, the client's mind and body become linked together to enjoy an experience that is powerful and opposite of the fragmentation with which he is familiar. Not only do the mind and body become connected, but the adult and child self become integrated. For the gay man who has spent a lifetime coping with shame and isolation, bringing back that young self is profound. As therapists, we can provide an experience in which the adult self befriends the child self.

Rather than continuing to hide in, the younger self is invited to come out too. And he will be welcomed and safe, as long as the adult is able to give him shelter and lead the way. Gay men sometimes avoid pain by not allowing visitations with their earlier selves. The fear of re-experiencing shame or feeling guilty precludes integration. The restricted, compartmentalized stance needs to be modified, which is why his treatment with you is crucial. The following brief case excerpt illustrates some of the deep modification that can be attained through hypnosis.

RON:

At 54 years old, Ron still feels the sting of having been criticized and misunderstood by his father. His father's voice still haunts him, and it drowns out his confidence.

With tears in his eyes he begins, "I connect with you (father) about my work ethic, but you never acknowledged how hard I worked. I see my business flourishing. Of course it is linked to what I learned from you, but I am always having to prove that I am worthy of respect."

I ask Ron to imagine his father during the last few years of his life. He sees his father sitting across from him: "Dad, you have changed." I decide to sit quietly rather than interrupt his powerful flow in trance. As I wait, I watch Ron's body transform. His posture shifts upward, he holds his head higher, the tears stop: "Warrior spirits. I just go on."

That was all he needed. I couldn't have made it any better by making interpretations or saying anything more. That moment was seared in his memory and landed in his body.

This shift prompted a spontaneous series of positive age regressions, where he goes back in time and recalls many positive memories.

He sees his favorite stuffed animal: "It is a dog with big floppy ears and nose, and it is soft. I am helping my mom with laundry and it feels good. She was my number one fan...." These and other images are being generated by him, not by me. This is a significant transformative moment.

Next, "I am in the tall grass near my house where I grew up. I am out in the open and hidden at the same time. (This is an interesting metaphor about being exposed, yet still hiding while he grapples with being gay.) The only noise is rustling grass. I feel peaceful. I am watching the clouds go by. It is a safe place."

Nature is often a place of refuge for clients who have experienced a tumultuous past. Since it provides serenity during hypnosis, I often encourage clients to imagine being in a place in nature.

Soon Ron moves to another place: "I am in the bedroom in my house. I am under my African sheets. I hang out there to be safe." As this theme of safety unfolds, he continues to spontaneously shift from one scene of safety to another. "It is a place to deal with my inner person [referring to his gay self]." Then, "These are good feelings, but feelings I knew I could never speak of back then. Now I live a life of openness. I do not need a protective cove anymore."

Script: Just Being You

So many of my clients spontaneously remember happy moments from their past, even without prompting. This is particularly important, since many people automatically discount their natural abilities. In this script I build on this.

Once clients are in a trance state, memories effortlessly come forward. I always ask clients to recreate these snippets of positive memory. Experiencing pleasure and having indirect reminders of inner strength fosters an appreciation of the significance of claiming one's own memories. A client's imagery is more powerful than imagery supplied to him.

Even clients with trauma histories are able to remember pleasurable moments. If you ask them to report about these memories out loud, you can amplify the experience by acknowledging their importance.

Begin with a basic relaxation or induction as outlined in Chapter Two. All experiential exercises are initiated with a short induction, or with a few moments where the sense of internal absorption is expanded upon.

> *You can remember a place in your past, perhaps for just a moment, or a series of moments, where you felt really content and comfortable. It may have been a safe place in your home, or perhaps a place outdoors in nature that you really enjoyed, or somewhere on vacation that was really special. Or perhaps you remember visiting somebody's house—perhaps the house of a relative or a good friend or a neighbor—and it felt really nice.*
>
> *You can really appreciate a moment where you felt really good and happy. You enjoyed the feeling of lightness inside. You were able to use your strength to either do well or feel really good. You were just being you.*
>
> *Notice and describe where it is that you are, and how old you are. What is it that you see as you look around—and is there anything you feel inside your body? You can also notice who else may have been there with you, and whether there are sounds, smells, or colors of which you are aware.*

Keep in mind that if your client is unable to retrieve positive memories or experience pleasure from doing this exercise, then he needs more basic stabilization.

BOYS WILL BE BOYS

"Gender cannot be seen apart from culture." (Hedges, 2011, p. 19) Expectations for both boys and girls stem from society. Boys should behave in certain ways—in school, neighborhoods, religious institutions, and most important in their families of origin. It is determined that simply because a child is a boy he will be and act in certain ways.

When a boy does not naturally meet certain expectations, there is a subtle interplay between a child and his parents (or whomever constitutes his family) about how he is different. Mostly unspoken, yet acknowledged from both sides, disappointment and fear may be the underlying feelings; disappointment that things are the way they are —different; and fear that the child will continue on this trajectory and life will be challenging for him.

My belief is that gay boys on some level always know they are gay. This is my own personal experience. Two common misconceptions about gay boys are that they are gay because they are too close to their mother, or because they were sexually assaulted by a man. Recently, while teaching a workshop, one of the participants bravely commented she had read that boys are gay because they were sexually abused by men. I was delighted when she continued by saying that she now realizes that she needs to change her thinking, and bring this new understanding to her patients and their families.

Wow! Think how this will change her work with clients. She can now support her clients and their families without having to wonder about abuse. She can be a bit lighter in her stance, less suspicious, and more optimistic in her approach.

To be okay with himself, a gay boy has, in addition to other things, to be ready to grieve that he is not like other boys or girls, and that he may be disappointing several people to whom he is close. Even worse, some family members or friends might consider him immoral or disgusting, or even dangerous.

He may know and not know he is gay at the same time. It is such a loaded issue. When he chooses to be fully aware of his sexuality and what it means that he is gay, he then has to decide whether to keep this secret or take the risk of sharing it. "How long have you been out?" can be a complicated question. The question might better be separated into two questions: "How old were you when you came out to yourself?" and "How old were you when you came out to others?"

"Free, spontaneous, and creative expression of ourselves in our personalities, and in our sexualities tends to become progressively curtailed as we continue to grow in relation to the demand of the sociocultural environment." (Hedges, 2011, p. 12) A child's healthy development includes an environment that encourages him to flourish, but the gay boy misses out on this basic need, therefore losing a sense of innocence. The pain of this will stay with him over the years.

This has become a central topic for gay psychotherapists who write about working with gay boys. "Gay men are severely oppressed by majority ideals. The boy learns to split off a certain essence of who he really is in order to fit in, and as a result, it is common to feel insecure and depressed." (Corbett, 2009, p. 111)

Sometimes a child is diagnosed as depressed when he is actually oppressed. The adult may then simply continue to carry the childhood diagnosis of depression into adulthood as becomes his self-definition. In the confusion along the way, opportunities for intimacy may be thwarted and relational complexities bypassed. Living concealed and being alone is an easier reality for some gay men.

In this short excerpt we connect some dots between what was and what could be.

HANK:

In a hypnosis session exploring his self-state of being incapable, Hank claims that his present limitations are linked with his lack of athleticism in seventh grade. "I told myself I could not play football. I felt incredibly self-conscious...the teacher was curt and humiliating."

He relates it to the present in saying, "All I felt was defeat and embarrassment. ...I was acquiescing and giving up, like I am now."

But immediately after Hank calls to mind athletes who can play sports well, he says, "I see and I feel one line of force and intention." I ask him to jump into the body of one of them to feel what he feels. He reports, "I feel joy. I know I can do it!"

Next, I ask Hank to implant this in himself for future situations in which he might experience fear. His body is pumped and excited. "I see a jump rope. This is a jump rope with electricity and liquid. It twists and leaps. I cross over it and under it. I jump forward with a huge leap. I jump away and I scream out, 'Yes, we are off to a good start! Let's keep it going. It will feel even better with more.' I know I can do it and will do it some more. I am not going to stop. I am not going to be a mummy anymore."

IT STILL ISN'T SAFE TO BE WHO YOU ARE

It is easier to be gay in the U.S. than ever before. We are no longer arguing (in most quarters) about whether or not gay men should be jailed, but rather whether or not traditional marriage should be extended to include same-sex couples.

Still, many clients coming to our offices are of an earlier generation and their internal experience is laden with conflict. Even today, there are relatively few gay male role models, and gay boys are left to find their own way in the world.

When I was around 6 years old, I was repeatedly caught playing with my sister's Barbie dolls, and my playing with her toys made her very upset. I don't think she was particularly disturbed to see me making outfits for the dolls, she just didn't want to share. My parents and my grandparents may have felt differently. Years later, when I was an adult, my mother told me that my grandmother was rather surprised by the endless hours I spent playing with my toy tea set.

Research by Richard Isay (Isay, 2009) reveals that gay boys of 4 and 5 years old felt different from their peers. They were more sensitive, cried more easily, and enjoyed aesthetic interests, such as nature, art, and music. They were often drawn to other sensitive boys, and were less aggressive. In addition, many were not interested in sports, and were made fun of by other kids. They were frequently humiliated, and often report they felt like an outsider.

Most of you reading this, especially if you are the parents of a gay boy, won't be at all surprised. Boys who are called sissies have few ways of expressing distress about being teased. Many protect themselves by hiding or rejecting the part of themselves that others might find objectionable. (Weiss, 2005)

I have sat with numerous clients whose parents sent them to therapy when they were kids, either because they were effeminate, or because they came out. Most were sent to therapists with the goal of conversion. Fortunately, these days, parental referrals for their children are increasingly made for acceptance and self-esteem rather than conversion or so-called reparation.

INTERNALIZED HOMOPHOBIA

The term "homophobia" is defined as having a negative view of homosexuality and homosexuals. Gay children who are fearful or homophobic may disown their own gay impulses and not act on them. As a way to fit it, they may also reject other kids who are gay. This may provide a façade of safety: being able to hide in order to avoid being rejected by peers.

Internalized homophobia runs deep. Extreme examples of internalized homophobia are men who live a traditional lifestyle in order to avoid being seen or identified as gay. Less extreme examples include self-consciousness about being in public, what to wear, and how or whether mannerisms may be perceived as feminine or gay. Every gay male, regardless of how long he has been out or how comfortable he is being gay, carries some form of internalized homophobia. One simply cannot grow up in a world that overwhelmingly reflects back a negative image—or no image at all—and emerge completely grounded in a confident, positive sense of self.

***

The following excerpt offers a glimpse of how a client's deep-seeded pain is quickly abated by a fresh experience of inner resources.

DANIEL:

Daniel is a 46-year-old gay man who is tired of not feeling good enough. His earliest memory of feeling different includes running around the house at age 3 wearing his mother's clothes. "Take that damned thing off. You are not a girl," yelled his dad.

From the age of 8 into his teens, he was repeatedly caught having sex by his parents. He was frequently punished, but being gay was never discussed.

"I kept trying to put these experiences out of my mind." (The cycle of experimenting and being caught, and then trying to put the shameful incident out of consciousness is common for many gay boys.)

"In seventh grade I really stood out. I dressed abnormally, compared to other teenagers, and I was bullied, verbally abused, ambushed, and pummeled by my classmates. They called me a fucking faggot and I internalized that shame. I told my best friend I could not hang out with him anymore. I guess it was out of self-protection, so I could find new friends. I frequently felt weepy and still now carry this inside of me."

It is indeed upsetting for me to sit with him as he tells his story. I want to find a way to take this pain away, yet I know I cannot. I also personally resonate with this story, based on my own experiences.

I recommend we try hypnosis to explore his awareness of resources and internal strength, suggesting that this is always a reliable way to enhance coping during painful moments in a session. After doing a brief induction, he reports: "I feel really, really, really calm, and I am loving this feeling. I am never able to relax like this, and now I can. I don't want to carry around darkness anymore. I am tired of that."

In subsequent sessions, we continue to use hypnosis to reinforce his ability to relax, to diminish the darkness, and most important, to explore his own optimism, which he had blocked so long ago.

ADOLESCENCE

Adolescence is a tough period, regardless of sexual orientation. The pressure to fit in and the scorn that people receive for being the slightest bit different can be downright cruel. Skin, weight, hair, clothes, family, athletic ability, scholastic achievement, friends, financial circumstances, and neighborhood are just some of the ways teenagers have to judge each other. They will do just about anything to fit in and be accepted. Until recently, and in many regions still, being gay would keep you out of almost any adolescent social clique.

For many, the ramifications of the isolation established in adolescence continue to bleed into adulthood. Children take responsibility for things that happen to them.

Corbett describes: "I have been called faggot or queer or sissy any number of times and with a variety of inflections. Mostly this naming occurred in my childhood. I venture that my peers were speaking to their perceptions that I was a proto-gay boy, but also to their experience of me as oddly able, and then again not, bookish, obsessive, artistic, too sensitive, reticent, verbally quick, physically quick as well, fast, and agile." (Corbett, 2009, p. 183)

Having repeatedly been made fun of myself, and having worked with innumerable gay men over the decades, it is clear that we all have our own personal stories of being called "faggot."

KENNETH:

Kenneth is a 35-year-old man, who struggles with career and financial success. As a result of his painful upbringing, his feeling ostracized continues into adulthood. His father had deserted the family when Kenneth was young, and he was raised by a single mother with limited financial resources. He regularly enjoys the benefits of hypnosis for self-actualization.

Here's an example:

"I see myself as a vulnerable third grader. I wasn't popular. I have memories of recess and feeling really lonely. I was always walking around by myself, watching other people play, but not participating. I felt different and I was always scared." (Watching people is often an important pastime for gay boys, in order to pick up cues on how to be and not to be.)

Knowing his capacity to use hypnosis to repair old self-images, I ask if he would like to go further. He nods and continues, "The floodgates are open, and I'm not holding back. All I feel is enthusiasm. I hear the usual old voice. 'You are the project kid. You are not deserving.'" He begins to weep. "Its presence is bothersome to me. I can jump out of this old mold and do my best from now on."

He keeps speaking, "This is so emotional!" Then the tears stop. His voice becomes deeper and stronger; his body is firm. "My ability to diminish shame and fear allows me to put them to rest."

He continues to flourish while in trance. "I see black and red butterflies flying off my back, flying away. I'm happy for me. It shakes loose so many things from back then. I've allowed the old memories of the projects to define my life in the present. I don't have to do this anymore." (The metaphor of butterflies may also reflect the struggle with being gay—one that he is able to shake loose.)

And then, as happens in hypnosis, something completely unexpected: He turns his head and speaks to his father as if he were there right in front of him, watching and listening: "Dad, I don't hate you. The only thing I want to thank you for is for giving me my life. I don't hate you. Really, I don't. You were not meant to be a good father. I get that now. The anger from the past is gone. It is unfortunate that you missed out on so many good things that make my life fulfilling. I feel peaceful. Now I am aware that there is no need to send energy into my anger anymore. It was not okay, but it is okay."

This is a good example of how hypnosis creates room for clients to come to themselves. If I, the therapist, had asked Kenneth to appreciate that his father had done the best he could, it would not have been nearly as powerful.

GAY BOYS AND THEIR FATHERS

Often gay men with whom I work felt estranged from their fathers growing up. As boys they knew they were not like their dads, and also that they were probably disappointing as sons. My clients tend to be aware of what they needed from their fathers—and of what they didn't receive.

Deep inside there's a sense of being flawed and bad, and the boy who is gay has to sort out not being male like his father, and not being female like his mother.

BUD:

Bud, a 47-year-old gay male, has struggled with obesity his entire life and has always felt great shame around being gay.

"As a kid, I had a very tumultuous relationship with my father. We were very, very different. I was studious. I liked to read. He was more of a sports person. And I felt stuck, no matter how much I tried to be good at sports to please him, I could not. I think I disappointed him and it put a wedge in our relationship even more."

"Even though he did not often call me a faggot, I know that is how he felt. I remember one time when I hurt myself and I went home crying, my father said, 'Men don't cry. Be a big boy, not a sissy.' So, at that point, I knew I had to deal with everything all by myself."

"One night when my father was drunk he did call me a faggot over and over again. I was heartbroken. My mother didn't jump in. I think she was afraid because he was drunk."

"I remember being about 9 or 10. My classmates called me a faggot and a fat pig, right before showering after gym. They beat me up. I just got feelings inside of me about wanting to die. That was the first time I ever had feelings that were this strong. I was not like anybody else out there and it felt like there was something wrong with me."

It seemed the right time for some experiential work. I decide to do some parts work with him. After doing a general induction, I gently ask if these parts can come out.

The incapable part:

"You cannot make decisions. Everything you have done you have made a mess out of. You cannot do it. You cannot be on your own. You are like a retarded boy who needs his mother and sisters to protect him. You need them or you will fall apart. You will always need help in this gloomy and dark place."

At this point Bud seems inconsolable. There are moments that I myself feel overwhelmed.

The okay part:

"It's okay. It's okay. You are gay; accept it. It's okay that you are gay." Then, "I can feel the guilt go out of me."

He continues: "You have every right to live just how you want to live. You have had enough sadness and you deserve happiness. It isn't your fault that you're gay. You're strong. You can do it."

His tears diminish and his voice becomes bolder. His eyes are still closed and his face is brighter: "I'm a good guy. I don't have to feel sorry for being alive anymore."

Then, when I ask him to imagine his father, he says, "Look at me. How I've come up in the family. I feel like I'm significant now. I accept my significance."

Age progression:

As he struggles about moving away from his parents' house, we spend time imagining him in the future living on his own.

"I am entertaining. I have people over, and I am okay without my parents. I can see myself working out, going to the gym, and calling people up. This is my place! Later, I see myself visiting my parents, just for a couple hours. This is so reassuring."

Later, when I ask about his bedroom, the magic continues to unfold. "I see a black bedroom set. Men with good taste in the city would buy the same one." He describes the bed, "I bought a queen mattress, based on the possibility of meeting someone and sleeping together in the future."

I chuckle and share the joy of that moment with him. Not only is he comfortable with the bold and masculine, but also the "queen" mattress.

He continues: "I am lying in my bed, and you know what? I am with a guy who is caressing me. We are just lying there, touching and caressing each other. I am not alone. I feel comfort. I do not want to lose this vision."

I ask him to look around the image to emphasize the power and the felt experience of the moment. "You will never believe this! I just saw this scene bounced back from the mirror in my bedroom set, where it was reflected twice!" Never would I have been able to create such a powerful moment for him. This is his creation.

MOTHERS

There is little research on gay boys and their mothers. Historical literature states that a mother's overinvolvement with her gay son is pathological, but I believe the opposite. Mothers have compensated for tension with the fathers. Often, their affection and love have been internalized by their sons and referenced in order to strive in the big cruel world. If the developmental task of a boy is to bond with his father and separate from his mother, where does that leave him when he is gay? So many clients have sat with me appreciating the bond they had with the one person who offered support. Corbett points out "... boys who can along with their mothers create a holding environment fare much better as they move into the outside world." (Corbett, 2009, p. 118)

If we can appreciate that the loving mother/son bond is a good bond and not pathologize that a boy may have some feminine traits, isn't this boy a little bit better off? Isn't the man he will become more likely to thrive?

Of course, religious perspectives, geographical location, and political views are among the variables that influence the messages children receive about what is normal and okay across many contexts.

The belief systems that are established and maintained seep into every aspect of the relationship between parents and children. Thus, the relationship between a gay son and his mother may be very complicated, even if deeply caring.

Many years ago I treated a Latina mother whose son was gay. She referred to "his illness." I often wondered what it meant for her son to be raised in this environment. Clearly, his mother loved him. His upbringing had many tender moments in his family and extended family, nevertheless he was still viewed as being sick.

I don't think I was able to provide the most effective interventions in this case. I was caught up in being a gay therapist working with a client who saw her gay son in a way that was challenging to me. I felt self-conscious because I had the same "illness" as her son, and was worried about her finding out about me. I felt like an imposter.

This type of interaction presents an interesting challenge for clinicians. It would be easy to feel critical of this mother. However, she also loved her son in wonderful ways, and was using her time in therapy appropriately by verbalizing her feelings.

Ideally, offering support around her painful dilemma of loving her son, despite his being gay, and educating her in a positive manner, would be the best approach. Countless examples could be offered of other religious mothers who have found a healthy way to compartmentalize their awareness of their sons' homosexuality in order to decrease stress and be able to carry on with their own lives.

If it was the other way around, and the therapist was working with the son, it would be easy to get caught up in loyalties to him and demonize his mother. The truth is, though he might take some solace in a therapist being critical of his mother, simultaneously he would find it hard, if not impossible, to tolerate it. We don't want to turn our clients against their parents or families. Ultimately, validating the dilemma that clients are experiencing, while providing possibilities and also keeping the pathways of communication open within the family, are the ingredients of optimal intervention.

WHAT YOU CAN DO FOR YOUR CLIENTS

As much as your adult client might think that he has evolved beyond his history and that these painful memories no longer dictate to him, old beliefs and vulnerability can be easily and quickly triggered. Being gay, feeling secretive, shame, and isolation, and being made fun of can all cause deep wounds. In time, they may fade, but the scars remain visible. There will be times when therapy can comfortably bypass history, and focus on the present. There are also times where pulling out old maps and revisiting the territory is the essential way to make true progress. Lightening the load by recognizing that the past is over and then finding a new route, can yield greater happiness

Using body awareness through experiential work, focusing on clients' resources, and using the strength of the therapy relationship is how change occurs. The following two scripts offer the metaphor of driving. As clients work on issues rooted in the past, the road ahead begins to unfold. This can be a felt sense, as well as piece of information. In this way, the idea of positive movement becomes accessible, knowable, and empowering.

Script: Bypass on the Highway

This script reminds people that they have choices when it comes to moving beyond their histories. Instead of dwelling in the past, there are ways of moving forward. The script emerged during my work with a client, who while still mired in the past, was on the threshold of stepping into the future.

> *You're traveling along a highway, approaching a town just ahead. Notice the variety of options available to you from the highway. You have the choice of going through this old historic town, or taking the older road that feels nostalgic, with many traffic lights, detours, and potholes. It takes you past familiar*

old buildings, some of which may be dilapidated and falling apart.

If you are in a hurry to get to your destination, it might frustrate you that you have chosen this slower route with its diversions and obstacles. A newer bypass road, one that is quicker with no need for stopping at lights or viewing old landmarks, is also available from the highway. That's right. You have the choice to enjoy your travel and reach your destination more quickly and easily. You can still have glimpses of the town on this bypass road and recognize its features, but you don't have to stop or be distracted.

Script: Rearview Mirror

Picture yourself in the driver's seat, driving in a car, down the road, looking into the rearview mirror. [Have the client notice or describe what the car looks like, smells like, etc. If you are working on a piece from his history, you can ask him to choose a car from that era.]

As you first look in the mirror, everything is close and you see it all so clearly. You even notice the small warning that says things in the mirror are, in this case, farther than they appear. As you continue traveling along, things that were up close are now farther and farther away. [Have the client expand on what he sees.]

Eventually, as you continue moving along this road, things that were right with you are no longer visible, they are farther and farther behind you now. You may remember what it is that you saw, and left behind. Even though the image may be remembered, you no longer see it. You no longer need to see it. It just recedes, farther and farther into the distance.

THINGS TO REMEMBER

As you work with a gay male client, help him to:

- Embrace the parts of himself that he loves from his past—activities, interests, or personality traits.
- Strike the right balance between the past and the present. Explore the past in order to live in the present with contentment.
- Enjoy the powerful experience of unity while doing work in trance.
- Maintain the focus on healing and growth. Demonizing others only reinforces anger and enmeshment.
- Befriend his child or adolescent parts, in order to receive nourishment.
- Expand his internal stance to find acceptance if not forgiveness with his family for the way he was treated. The fuller the present, the softer the gaze toward the past.

CHAPTER FOUR

The Therapy Relationship: Experience Expansion— Expand Experience

Last chapter's focus on development reminds us that, in general, gay men have grown up feeling diminished in their families and in society. The way in which they interact in the world is shaped by these experiences and so the stakes are high when they come see you. Comfort and compassion are essential components in successful treatment with gay men, and the immediate goal is to create a positive alliance. Growth takes root in this alliance, regardless of which therapeutic models or specialties you offer.

Because connection takes precedence in the moment, paperwork that comes with this professional interaction can be put aside in favor of establishing rapport. Paperwork can wait; connection cannot.

When the client shows up to your office for psychotherapy, he will already be in a vulnerable state. His presenting issue, which is often a source of failure or shame, is accompanied by the internalized feeling that being gay is to blame. Thus, the association formed by the two of you must serve as a foundation for ongoing trust, in order to explore what inherently feels dangerous.

SIZING YOU UP

Gay male clients will be sensitive to certain aspects of interaction with you and sensitive to your particular qualities. Gay men are well versed in detecting safety concerns.

- Do you understand him?
- Are you reassuring?
- Do you accept him being gay?
- If you do, are you conveying it in a way that feels accepting and loving?
  (If he is coming to therapy based on issues pertaining to sex, intimate relationships or compulsive behaviors, this will be especially salient.)
- If you are gay, do you share enough similar viewpoints for the relationship to feel safe and satisfying?
- Is there a way in which the fact that you are gay actually evokes a sense of competition in him?
- Are you the kind of gay man with whom he feels comfortable—a therapist who understands his values within the community?
- Is your style something he judges you for, or reacts to?
- If you are not gay, what are your biases, and how or when will they show up?
- Are you open enough?
- Whatever your orientation, do you offer the right balance of familiarity, professionalism, and freshness?

As I said, the first goal at the start of new treatment is to make the connection. Remember the gay male's history. Your client's needs may have him looking outside of himself for acceptance, and your job at the beginning is a tough one. It is easy to fool ourselves into thinking we are doing what is right in order to make a connection, but paying attention to subtle interactional qualities is a crucial aspect of creating that necessary sense of trust. Dr. Zeig asks clinicians to imagine themselves in the consulting room: "What postures do you habitually assume? Are you unnecessarily rigid? What flexible postures can you adopt that can enhance your effectiveness?" (Zeig, 2006, p. 2)

If the client has been in therapy before, his explanation of, "I wanted something new," may warrant some exploration. Does he have a sense that his previous therapist disapproved of aspects related to him being gay? Did he come to some kind of therapy impasse? Was he having trouble translating insight into action? Whatever the reason for his having left the previous context, you're it now, and in order to meet him where he is, you will need to appreciate his dilemma, figure out his relational style, and provide the right amount of what he needs.

Keep in mind that most gay men are used to sitting on the sidelines. Showing sincere enthusiasm is inspiring, though it may take some time for him to adjust to the attention. Most clients come to therapy wanting to resolve a problem. Some are clear that it is crucial to have a good connection with the therapist in order to accomplish this, but others may not be aware of the importance of this aspect of therapy.

Most gay men have grown up in unempathic environments. Thus, empathic resonance and responsiveness from the therapist are of particular importance. At the same time, the therapist's empathic responses may fall on deaf ears as the client questions the genuineness of the interaction. (Cornett, 1993)Gay males suffering from low self-esteem are accustomed to deflecting energy from themselves and may have a knack for not accepting positive feedback. I also attribute the reaction to internalized homophobia (mentioned in the previous chapter). People with low self-esteem are more comfortable with critical feedback than praise, and they elicit values that confirm their negative self-view. (Short, 2010)

A quick story: A client who is not new to therapy but has just joined a group I lead reveals the tenaciousness of low self-esteem, even as one is receiving very positive feedback. This man is upbeat, attractive, articulate, and warm. When it is pointed out by the group that he exhibits these traits, his face becomes flushed, he breaks eye contact, looks down, and his posture transforms into that of a vulnerable child. Exploration of this response only brings out more embarrassment and shame. This is a man who is successful in business and to whom others respond with interest. His mysteriousness—a façade developed to hide behind—only evokes greater interest. In this moment, the uncertainty that lurks just beneath the surface is glaring.

ATTUNEMENT

As therapists, we always appreciate the significance of the therapeutic relationship or we wouldn't be working in this field. The topic is endlessly captivating. "The therapy relationship is more than a staging ground for technique; it is the primary factor in successful psychotherapy." (Short, 2010, pp. 3-4) Our chief goal is to provide a meaningful experience to our clients. It is that simple. For gay men, this meaningful experience provides the greatest opportunities for change. Remember, using body awareness through experiential work, focusing on clients' resources, and using the strength of the therapy relationship creates optimal change.

You and your client will simultaneously enjoy the rewards of using this three-prong approach. Attunement refers, in part, to this palpable shared experience. The term "attunement" has become popularized, based largely on remarkable neuroscientific findings. Mutual physiological changes take place when people are attached to and are in sync with each other. (Yapko, 2012)

YOUR NATURAL SELF

Whether a client was referred to you because of your areas of expertise or because of your reputation, being appreciative of the dynamic of the relationship is crucial. How you exhibit warmth and interest in him makes a difference. It is your natural strengths that create the greatest comfort and promote closeness. How you interact is far more important than the exact words you use. Techniques that you learn are helpful, but perfecting them might be more significant for you than for your client. Your stance is that of a healer: respectful and sacred in your intentions. You are an important figure to your client, perhaps in ways he has never experienced in his life before.

Literature delights in affirming the significance of this relatedness. Successful therapy depends much more on the connection, empathy, and mutual fondness that develop between a gay client and therapist than any other attribute of the therapist. "What is healing is the client experiences being at one with the therapist." (Stark, 1999, p. 200)_It is more important that the therapist direct efforts toward appreciating the client's experience than focusing on what really happened. This perspective centers on the client's affective experience. (Stark, 1999, p. 196)

In our current work with gay men, we can also explore sensory experiences. This opens up a treasure chest of possibilities because somewhere within him are his resources. Perhaps they have been dormant for years, but with caring guidance they can be elicited from deep inside. Research indicates that within the context of healthy relationships, individuals are able to gain experience of identity, meaning, choice, and love. The combination of these produces hope and resiliency. We discover our value, stretch our limits, gain new abilities, and collaboratively create a meaning for our existence. (Short, 2010, pp. 301, 302) Authenticity opens to creativity and collaboration; the powerful mixture leads to success in the therapy.

Attunement in Action

- Create an inviting, informal atmosphere.
- Make eye contact with your clients.
- Be aware of your body language and show yourself to be open and welcoming.
- Use your intuition to create a relational match by joining the client in his ways of perceiving things and living life.
- Trust the unique ways in which information comes to you as you sit with your client. Utilize them.
- Use humor with purpose in order to promote closeness or emphasize a point.
- Strive to make a powerful connection that is profoundly experienced by both of you.
- Focus on experience rather than technique.

AUTHORITY FIGURES

For gay men positive experiences with authority figures are few and far between. Most gay men have concealed their identity or behaviors, recognizing there was always the danger that people in positions of authority would be disapproving. I still find that many clients don't tell their physicians they are gay, despite being sexually active. They are afraid their physician will react negatively, and the need for interpersonal harmony surpasses anything else. Of course, it is of the utmost importance to maintain good physical health, get regular HIV tests and immunizations for hepatitis, and to have safe sex discussions. If a physician or therapist is perceived as being disapproving, the option of another provider is always a good one, yet secrecy is the default mode for many men. They forget that they have other options. This scenario happens just as often in psychotherapy, especially where sex and use of substances are concerned.

WHAT DOES IT MEAN TO BE GAY AFFIRMATIVE?

I have highlighted that gay male clients flourish through your ability to notice and utilize their resources. This is the magic you can easily provide. Although it isn't difficult, it is often forgotten amidst the therapy protocols and the current emphasis on identifying treatment goals. Clients are the best at self-pathologizing. Gay liberation itself is still fairly young (early 1970s); affirmative therapy for gay males is even younger.

Before 1990, there was ample literature to support the idea that conversion from homosexual to heterosexual was a preferred intervention. Some therapists believed it was in the best interest of their clients to change their sexual orientation, given that it is impossible for a gay man to live a happy life or have a stable relationship. (Isay, 2009) There is still conservative religious literature that supports this perspective, but it is less common than before.

There is now consensus that it is damaging to a gay man to attempt reparative or conversion therapy. (Isay, 2009)I am surprised at how often I get referrals of men who were treated with conversion as the goal. However, more common these days than outright suggestions for conversion, is the perception of disapproving attitudes from psychotherapists that negatively reinforce a client's feeling about being gay. Often these therapists are seen as rejecting and uncaring (Isay, 2009), though I would guess that many of them are actually just unaware of how they are coming across to their clients. People who grow up with healthy authority figures may not recognize that a gay man has tended to the needs of the authority figures (including parents) in his life by keeping quiet and hiding his secrets. Therefore, a client may recreate in therapy a dynamic he had with his parents by remaining hidden. The need to be compliant or good prevails. Therapists need to be on the lookout for such a dynamic and create a tone that implies mutual openness and acceptance.

The bottom line is that accepting your client for being gay is essential. A wonderful description of gay-affirmative therapy states: "Psychotherapy can result in change, although this is the secondary goal to creating an experience of empathic contact for the patient, whether or not change takes place." (Cornett, 1993, p. 61) Right on! Making this connection will be as useful as anything else.

Perhaps the best way to provide affirming therapy is to accept and affirm that you care for your client. Then you find a way to join him in his views and sensibilities. The therapist's ability to be reliable provides a milieu that aids the patient in experiencing "twinship." Sensitivity and empathy affirm that patient's sense of self. (Cornett, 1993, p. 54)Internalization of these interactions can lead to significant internal structural expansion and cohesion.

A GAY-AFFIRMATIVE PERSPECTIVE IN ACTION

You want your client to feel comfortable, valuable, proud about being gay, and for him to know that you are in accord with his true self. You can do this by finding avenues of connection with him, as a person, not just as a client.

Allow yourself to appreciate how you respect him, where your commonalities intersect, and how your differences are intriguing to both of you. This way of relating is not didactic, rather it is intuitive and emotional. Either you both feel it, or you don't. There is no need to try too hard to win him over; the way that you effortlessly relate is the win.

Script: Seeing and Knowing You

This script was inspired by a client sharing his difficult experiences of coming out in college. Because these struggles were having an effect on his coursework, his professor asked to meet to offer him support. His memory of receiving nurturance all those years ago was so profound that he describes it as a turning point in his life. Ironically, he remembers nothing about what was said. Instead, he vividly recalls the feeling of being cared for in this special relationship. The lamp that was shining on his professor's desk figures prominently in his memory. The visual representation of this lamp still captivates him and represents the richness of this experience, even 30 years later.

I am struck by how other clients report similar types of childhood or young adult memories, often with neighbors, grandparents, aunts, uncles, or other people who shared their love.

This script can be used as a reminder that there were people in the past whose nurturance made a lifetime of difference. In addition, I use this script at conferences and with therapists to remind them of significant moments like this in their own past.

For traumatized clients who cannot conjure up anyone who provided this type of experience, a family pet or a childhood toy can be used.

Allow a time in your past to come to you when you may have felt awkward, just a little bit different from others, or per-

haps you felt alone. It might have been as a child or as a teenager, and you can look back and appreciate what it was like for you then, remembering the ways that you may have held yourself back, or constrained yourself. You can even assume that position in your body right now.

You can also appreciate how time has shifted for you now, since you are no longer in that place anymore.

Now, remember a person back then who could see you and know you for who you really were, and for what you needed at that moment in time. You can appreciate how it feels that you knew that he or she cared about you; how lucky you were and are to know that he or she cared. This caring person may not have even verbalized the ways that he or she could appreciate you, or the ways that you mattered, but you just knew this was so. You simply knew this by the way the person looked at you, spoke to you, or did something special, just for you. Appreciate the way it feels inside.

It may have been a teacher, a doctor, an aunt or uncle, or perhaps a neighbor who noticed you and took care of you in just the right ways. In your mind, you can see what this person looks like, where you were back then, and what the surroundings looked like. You might even remember the sounds or smells. That is right.

This person could see you for who you really were and really are, and was able to offer you love and support and it felt so very special. It was just what you needed. Appreciate how it feels now and assume that position in your body. That is right.

"IF I CAN, SO CAN YOU."

I provide experiences that help my clients feel alive through my own interactive stance. Near the start of treatment I say: "What you see is what you get." In addition, I am mindful of my posture, movements, tone of voice, and use of eye contact—all to imply an available informal stance that encourages the same of them. This mindset offers gay men new opportunities. It is met with great relief, especially for clients who in the past have had more aloof therapists. Clients are grateful to experience this positive energy and it elicits a new way of being. My informal use of self serves as a role model with its intrinsic message of acceptance of being gay. Just being myself has proven to be the most successful therapeutic tool in the room. Again, behind the curtain of any therapy technique should be authenticity. This is what allows for the power of any given technique to come through.

A quick story about my client, Thomas: He was raised Mormon and says he envies the confidence of his Jewish friends. Turns out, his therapist, me, is Jewish and gay. I was excited from the start that he was willing to use the energy between us as a part of therapy; it is just how I love to work.

While exploring career stagnation, he describes a scene in hypnosis that suggests a dynamic between us. It hadn't occurred to me until months later when I reread my notes that the person he described might be me. It reflects how powerfully the relationship in therapy is experienced, even when it isn't in full conscious awareness.

"There is a man in the foreground, standing in water. It is some kind of a pond or a lake. There is a reflection of a forest behind him, and the background is green and black. The sun is focused on this man. He is smiling with his head tilted, looking friendly, but strong and inviting."

Perhaps the sun that focuses on me symbolizes the success my client perceives in me, or me in him. I am often inviting him to leap into the depths of the water, either with me, or by himself.

***

The next excerpt brings Brad back. Here you get a glimpse of what the weave of therapeutic alliance, experiential work, and calling forth the client's resources looks like in session.

BRAD:

Thinking about his growth in therapy, Brad is very clear: "Love is wanting someone who truly wants me, rather than my settling for his approval of me. I have been waiting too much for permission from men. I deserve to have a man offer me what it is that I want, and it is exciting that I am beginning to be self-directed now. I am going against the old voices I have lived with for years."

In exploring ongoing themes, he describes, "When I am faggy, I am faggy by choice. No more editing of myself!"

Knowing how much he enjoys being creative in hypnosis, I decide to embrace his "faggy" stance in a way that symbolizes resourcefulness. I ask him to describe a memory when feeling this way was wonderful. (This was all with his eyes closed, in hypnosis, where he could let himself go more than usual.) He recalls going to a disco in the late '70s: "Everybody was happy, celebrating their gayness and having a ball on the dance floor, uninhibited and free."

When I ask which "faggy" song was playing—reflecting back his use of the word "faggy" in a light and easy way—he answers: "'I Feel Love' by Donna Summer." Since we grew up in the same era, we spend a few moments mutually sharing our enjoyment of these times. I continue with this theme.

I ask him to bring this feeling of being free to a time in his past when he would have liked or needed more of it.

"I am way in the back of my parents' station wagon. This was a place where I would go to in order to escape from them, and try my best to feel free from them."

Knowing that he is a wonderful singer, and assuming that his singing will be a powerful experiential moment, I then ask him to sing the song out loud. I am right. It becomes a powerful and intimate moment. I push him to push himself further than he usually does, and I also participate in enjoying the depths of the intimate moment, one of the more intimate moments in my career.

He begins meekly:

Ooh
It's so good, it's so good
It's so good, it's so good
It's so good
Ooh
You and me, you and me
You and me, you and me
You and me
Ooh
It's so good, it's so good
It's so good, it's so good
It's so good
I feel love, love, love, love,
I feel love

He is very self-conscious, but he continues. It is incredible. I ask him to describe what happens next. "You are driving the car, the music is blaring, I am way in the back and the lights are blinking, like the lights in the disco. We are now at a red light, where the people in other cars watch us."

He is emphatic: "Turn up the volume, Rick!"

I had turned up the volume by asking him to sing, and gladly turn up the volume again in this important moment.

With tears, he says, "This is so incredibly hard. I want to be somewhere where all of this is okay, and it is right here."

EXPERIENCES UNITE

The success you achieve with your clients comes from your ability to join your client in his world. This often feels like a trance state or state of flow where everything else goes away and it is just the two of you. This ability to join involves the challenging task of putting your own perceptions and experiences aside. However, in a trance state it can feel effortless. Martha Stark describes the tension between decentering, in order to lose herself in the client's experience, and recentering, in order to give her authentic self to her client. (Stark, 1999, p. 199) Though she does not do hypnosis, it certainly is hypnotic.

A client sitting with his eyes closed and allowing the therapist to guide his experience is in a vulnerable position. (Yapko, 2011) In that moment, the client is no longer able to reference the therapist's facial expressions to judge how the emotional interaction is proceeding. (Brown, 1986) Trust is paramount and should be well established before embarking on this type of work, and one should only proceed with the client's full permission.

The payoff for those who can establish comfort with vulnerability is that therapist and client together have greater access to the richness of the client's internal world. This happens through joint exploration and joint experience. Clinician and client follow each other's leads, and at the same time, each takes the lead. (Yapko, 2011)

The experience is mutual: a deep state that is creatively assembled and experienced with and for each other. This is interpersonal trance. The therapist's unconscious mind tunes into the client's unconscious messages, feelings, and needs. The therapist involved in this trance activity is better able to resonate empathetically with the client, and to meet his unconscious needs. As both experience a receptive trance, the client is also experiencing an interactive, interpersonal state of high resonance. The internal resources of therapist become available to him. (Frederick, 1999)

Even though this is done experientially, the experience is processed consciously, and the client not only has the benefit of what came up while doing this work, but also has the benefit of expanding on the respectful and loving experiences within him.

Often, while doing hypnosis, I am aware that I am talking to the child, and that he is responding to me, both as child and as adult. Thus, during these moments, I exaggerate the softness or the kindness in my voice. The client is often nodding his head, receiving my voice —its cadence and tone—as though listening to a lullaby. Inevitably, the experience of being understood and appreciated frequently moves clients to tears. Milton Erickson believed that the therapist's role is to be a surrogate parent, and I concur.

The following brief excerpt provides a snippet from a much longer hypnosis session in which I placed emphasis on being relational and tailoring to build on the solidity of my connection with the client.

BUD:

As mentioned in Chapter Two, Bud was having difficulty moving out of his parents' home and establishing an independent life. Together we go on a journey, traveling by car.

Me: And even though I am driving the car, I wouldn't know where to go unless you gave me directions, because you are the navigator and all I am doing is following your directions.

Bud: We are still in the car. You are continuing to drive me past all the dark places. And you know exactly where to go, you know where to take me. I can't do this alone. Please don't leave.

Me: And you can trust Bud that I am here for you. That I am not going to drive away. And I wonder if you can appreciate moments when you sit here with me during a session, and moments when you leave a session and I am not with you anymore, and yet I am with you at the same time.

Bud: *[Nodding his head]* That feels very manageable, very reassuring. Not so scary. Manageable. It doesn't feel as scary, or lonely. I can hear you in the back of my mind telling me I can do this, I can manage this. It feels good. It makes me feel like I can do this. I can hear you saying 'You can do this, you can get through this.'

"I AM HERE FOR YOU"

Earlier, I talked about the significance of maintaining a "you can" position for our clients. Another important stance is "I am here for you."

I say or imply this often, and with great sincerity. When offered at the right moments it cuts through many protective layers. Sometimes I directly say this in hypnosis. If a client is struggling with pain, I want him to know that he doesn't have to hold it by himself. This is a hard allowance for men who have been denied and have denied themselves the availability of others, and love.

JASON:

Jason is a client with a painful history of sexual abuse, alcoholism, physical abuse, and emotional neglect. He has learned to quietly excel in his own private world. Although it appears that he is successful and gregarious and has many close friends, he is actually a loner and keeps himself well hidden from others.

Over the course of his sessions, it is clear that he is doing with me what he does with others: deflecting and hiding. One day I decide to take a big risk.

I ask him if he knows that I am really there for him. Tears come to his eyes. "I am here for you, Jason. And I will continue to be here for you." These words are magic to him. He continues to weep, relieved and moved.

Later, he expressed many times that this was a pivotal moment in his life. "It was the first time I could believe the truth of this: Rick is and was there for me."

GOING DEEPER INTO THE RELATIONSHIP: DEALING WITH CONFLICT

- When you sense that your client is having a struggle with you, do you encourage him to speak about it?
- Do you ask him to describe what he needs from you?
- Are there times when you avoid these kinds of conversations?
- Do you find yourself giving in to your fear about pushing your client?

- How many times has your client had struggles with an authority figure and not been able to discuss it?

Many of us simply prefer to avoid these kinds of discussions and instead focused solely on the client's symptoms and presenting problem. In doing this, we miss out on rich moments. We hope that the connections with our clients provide lasting change, and that our relationship provides the love of a parental figure. It does, and yet there needs to be more; working through the resolution of conflict is a crucial piece. It adds richness to the therapeutic experience, particularly with clients who stay for longer treatment.

Dealing and working through conflict, in the context of the therapy relationship, is a must because a gay client's history with conflict may simply consist of avoidance. But in life, conflict is inevitable; now is his chance to move through it in a different way. The question is: Will you meet him there?

WHOSE FAULT IS THIS ANYWAY?

Apologies and countertransference disclosers are crucial to successful therapy with gay men. The shame that gay clients feel is often manifested in accepting responsibility for painful experiences that are externally prompted. An empathic lapse by the therapist often becomes a source of self-criticism for the client. (Cornett, 1993)

I recall once in a group I was leading that I made a joke which turned out to be at the expense of one of the participants. As soon as I blurted out the joke, the group came to Todd's rescue, making clear that my comment was too gruff. It would have been tempting to rush to my own defense, "explaining" what I really meant, in order to save face. Of course, this would have also further isolated the participant and put the group in a dilemma.

Instead, I contacted him immediately following the meeting and apologized. And, in the next meeting I took responsibility by reiterating to the group what Todd and I had talked about. It was important for the group, and Todd verified how important it was for him to have me apologize.

Martha Stark discusses "The New Good –The Old Bad"—the unconscious wish on the client's part to engage the therapist in a reenactment of his internal dramas. The therapist is assigned the position of the powerful parent—a position that at times the client once had as a vulnerable child in relation to his powerful parent. (Stark, 1999) "Good is internalized as a consequence of surviving the experience of being failed." (Stark, 1999, p.31) Keeping this in mind can be a useful way of reminding ourselves why it is important to understand the client's needs, rather than simply defending our actions. The goal is to have a resolution of relational difficulties through reworking "bad."

My insensitivity in the form of a joke made Todd feel shame, and being able to own this allowed him to not to blame himself. Job poorly done (the joke), and then well done (the apology).

Again, Stark: "A truly empathic perspective is never an issue of who is right, or who is wrong. Rather, what matters is the client's perception, the perception of having been failed." (Stark, 1999, pp. 191,192)_She further describes the inevitability of conflict in the therapeutic relationship, and refers to a "corrective provision" that needs to happen, hence, the new good. The emphasis is not so much on intellectual understanding, but on emotional experiencing. (Stark, 1999, p. 28)

Script: The Calm After the Storm

Frequently, after a disagreement, there is uncertainty or tentativeness in any relationship. Based on the significance of the therapeutic relationship, when a client is willing to stay in therapy after a conflict, we want to reassure him (and ourselves) that things can and will be okay again. Even though we know that working through conflict is essential, gaining confidence afterward is also important. This can be healing for the client and therapist, and serves as a reminder about the importance of the mutual relationship.

You can appreciate that when there is a heavy rainstorm just how loud and intense it seems. As you listen to the sound of the rain beating on the ground or the building in which you are seeking refuge, it seems as though the storm is never going to end. Roads or walkways get flooded, plants get beaten down, and that unsettling feeling inside feels endless.

However, there is always a time when the storm abates. You know that from your own life experiences, yet in the midst of it, it seems as though the waiting is endless.

Sometimes summer storms are the most intense. You can watch the sky turning darker and darker, with the winds getting heavier, and then, the rain comes.

But, as quickly as it appears, it also passes with the same speed and the gusto. Sometimes you can see the sky split between darkness and light. Not only do you know that the light and the sun will reappear, you await it. That is right.

Appreciate that really calm feeling in your body as the rain stops and you see the sun coming out again. Everything is brighter, quieter, and even the birds quickly start chirping again. Notice the ways in which things shine as the sun reappears. That is right.

When you were a kid, or when you were on vacation, you might have even ventured outdoors after the storm to walk around. Walking barefoot, feeling the warmth from the earth or pavement on your feet, seeing the mist rise from the ground, and taking in those post rain smells. It feels so quiet and so calm now, so different from just a few moments before. Really appreciate the ways in which your body absorbs the calmness and the quietness. The worst is over., You now feel a quiet and a peace inside. Excellent.

THE OTHER SIDE OF THE COIN

If the relationship is at the center of successful therapy, what happens when the relationship doesn't hold? Like many therapists, I have had this experience.

DAVID:

David's initial reasons for coming to therapy involved social anxiety and depression, which kept him from developing friendships and intimate relationships with other gay men, which he craved. For months our relationship was wonderful. I was the stand-in for a good enough parent, chiefly his father. Interestingly, when he would visit his father, he would return and be more reticent with me. It was as though he were being forced to choose between us—his rigid father and the more accepting figure he found in me—and rather than choose, he simply shut down until we were able to once again open our communication.

Our sessions were very satisfying. We spoke at length about his family and the significance of his independence. We also spoke about his social involvement in gay sports and the local gay gym as ways of meeting people. He slowly took risks and began to develop his social confidence.

When he felt ready to take on a new challenge, we agreed that a gay interpersonal therapy group would be the next step for him.

But at a certain point, he became angry with the group and with me for not having protected him in the way that he wanted.

This was painful for me. I was accustomed to being his savior, and knowing some of his self-destructive impulses, such as drinking or isolating himself, had me worried. I contacted him and asked him to agree to come in for at least one session before making any final decisions.

I practiced and practiced what I would say. I also got some supervision and coaching. I wrote him letter and I read out loud to him. This showed David how much time and care I put into thinking about him. It also allowed me to say what I needed to say without getting sidetracked. Yes, I wanted him to grow, but I also wanted us to be okay.

I wrote: "Thank you for your willingness to be honest, contemplative, and truthful. Can you hear my viewpoint, experience my judgment and trust that I still care about you? Can you give yourself the gift of experiencing a disagreement and love at the same time? Do you accept that I (unlike your father) can tolerate your outbursts and still embrace you? Can you use your heart, rather than your hurt and your pain to make a decision? Can you stick with the relationships that bring you love, recognition and feeling understood?"

David melted with tenderness. Our mutual stalemate loosened up. Experiencing me as the old bad, David would have fled from treatment, and almost did. But with hard work, he allowed the opportunity for the new good, and as a result, was able to stay in therapy with me.

Sadly, a couple of years later another conflict occurred and David left treatment without our being able to mend our frayed edges.

In hindsight, I realize that by constantly defending myself, I inadvertently chipped away at the empathy that David needed from me. He knew this and continued pointing it out, yet I kept defending my stance, which in the long run broke the connection. However, in understanding this now, and no longer hanging on to the need to defend myself, there is a kind of reconnection too. It is my hope that he also finds this and can reclaim what he received from our work together.

Script (for therapists): Reclaiming Your Balance

This script is used to remind us, as therapists, that we have our unique abilities to care for our clients in ways that are intimately and mutually experienced. However, when we get stuck in a struggle with our clients, or when they get stuck in a struggle with us, we sometimes forget that as therapists we can often make the shift that promotes closeness. This is a satisfying reminder of the implicit bond that exists between therapist and client.

> *Allow a client with whom you sometimes struggle come into your awareness. Remind yourself that the love that comes*

from warmth and acceptance is what makes you a good therapist in your own unique and special way. That is right. Allow yourself to fully experience this inside now.

Notice the shift that you may experience as you visualize yourself sitting with this person. Feel it inside yourself, and notice how it may have shifted from the previous client with whom you do not struggle.

In this moment, you can really appreciate the ways in which uncertainty is experienced, perhaps by both of you. Be aware of tightness or tension inside, and how you may communicate this to your client, even in ways that may not be direct, or in ways that aren't even verbalized. That is right.

Sometimes it is hard to acknowledge this, yet this time it may be just a bit easier to appreciate how you, as the unique therapist that you appreciated moments ago, can be available in a new or different way to this client with whom you struggle.

Even though it is hard, you can visualize yourself looking or sitting differently with this client. You can take this moment of feeling centered and bring it into the therapy session with this client. That is right.

Something about this moment right now allows you to acknowledge that there may be ways that you can carry yourself differently with your client, and you can even allow yourself to see a slight shift in the session between the two of you, all because you are able to find the strength inside of you to make a shift. And each time you make a shift like this, a change is felt between you, even though it may be little by little. Each change creates success.

As you see and feel this change taking place, just notice the ways in which you look different, feel different, and are different, both inside and out. Good. You can bring this with you, inside of yourself to future sessions. You can enjoy the ways that you experience love and acceptance.

We all do our best and want to be the kind of therapist who makes a big difference in our clients' lives. We work toward making an alliance that will be profound. We don't want there to be misunderstanding, but sometimes it happens. It is best to be honest—this is what we guide others to do.

Sometimes our defenses, needs, or vulnerabilities keep us from finding the right ways to settle the difficult moments. It is up to us to discover paths to achieve resolution. If this is not possible, there is always the option of another therapist who may be better suited to a particular client. Often verbalizing the truth of a struggle is more helpful than anything else, and being honest about parting ways is easier than sifting through continual conflict, or acting as though everything is fine when you both know it isn't.

FINALLY… DOES A GAY MALE CLIENT NEED A GAY MALE THERAPIST?

It's all about relationship, right? A client needs to feel safe, seen, accepted, and understood. The therapist also needs to feel these things so that he or she can create an environment that promotes them. Generally, I have found that heterosexual male therapists are more homophobic than female therapists. Many gay men would agree with this, which is why they might be hesitant to work with heterosexual men.

I am careful about who I refer to whom. Even though referrals are frequently geographically determined, I am always careful to ascertain whether the therapist I am referring to is gay affirmative. With people I don't know, I ask about their experiences working with gay men, and then listen closely to what they say and how they communicate with me. What I feel inside is most important, as if I were pursuing a therapist for myself. If I feel discomfort, I find another referral. I pride myself on making meaningful referrals and I suggest you do the same.

Having a heterosexual therapist who is loving can be rewarding in many ways. Being accepted by a straight person is more powerful than being accepted by a gay man because of the painful histories with authority figures discussed earlier. Internalizing these experiences can mark the beginning of a new relationship with authority beyond therapy and into life.

If you are not gay, your gay clients will carefully and quietly assess your comfort level with them. This includes your knowledge about the gay community and what gay people experience in their day-to-day lives, internally and externally. It also matters how you communicate this. Transformational relationships require sensitivity to differences and flexibility in responding to these differences. (Short, 2010) If you don't know much about the gay community and feel comfortable acknowledging this, your sincerity will be perceived in a positive way. Pretending, on the other hand, will be detected and perceived as rejecting. Sometimes a heterosexual therapist who doesn't understand the gay culture will express judgment, which is hurtful, especially because gay men have repeatedly had this experience. Skilled therapists do not challenge clients' core beliefs. (Short, 2010)

The Four Pillars of Relationship Building

- *Honesty:* Be truthful about the extent of your experience in working with gay clients, no matter how limited. Your client will respond to your willingness to tell the truth. It's the beginning of trust.

- *Authenticity Trumps Knowledge*: Success in therapy is rooted in meaningful connection. Attention to the relationship is even more important than attention to your tools.

- *Being Yourself*: Gay men are especially sensitized to you being who you are (deception equals danger for gay men). And isn't this the point of therapy: to be okay with who you are?

- *Therapeutic Interactions*: Your love and acceptance are the wellspring of his growth and healing.

CHAPTER FIVE
The Myth of the Urban Gay Man

The life of an urban gay man is not easy, although the media has gone from pathologizing it to romanticizing it. With a powerful history of becoming invisible in order to be safe and of feeling on the outside of whatever group there was, adulthood doesn't automatically mean that these internalized norms disappear; psychotherapeutic work is usually an imperative.

In addition, the urban gay community has some tough rules itself. There are common expectations that put everyone under a great deal of pressure. There is an etiquette and hierarchy that must be negotiated. In other words, the gay boy has made it to adulthood only to find an all new club in which to feel outsider and not good enough. For some, it's better to continue to be invisible than to be visibly less than. So much for easy.

Within the gay male world, the widely accepted stereotype includes specific standards: where to live, how to dress, what to look like, and how to behave. Most gay men chase this perfect "A-list" fantasy.

Huh, Why?

- Why does a gay man buy into this stereotype?
- Does he really enjoy chasing these standards?
- Is it that he experiences a sense of belonging that takes away the old historical loneliness?

- How is this sense of belonging felt consciously and unconsciously?
- What price does he really pay in order to fit in?

When I discuss my work at teaching conferences, I present a slide show depicting the urban gay male stereotype. There is dance music and images of successful urban gay men: muscular, ripped, handsome, young, and usually white, with a beautiful apartment, beach home, and expensive cars. Of course, he is hanging out at bars or parties with similarly gorgeous gay men!

I make light of this stereotype, but make no mistake, it weighs heavily on many gay men, even if they are not aware of it.

"I FEEL HORRIBLE ABOUT HOW I LOOK."

Your client undoubtedly feels awful about his physical appearance. This has little to do with the reality of how he looks. His face and/or his body don't measure up. He imagines that his belly is too big, his penis is too small, his hair is the wrong color--all of this deemed by the media as being unacceptable. By the time he is an adult, the gay man has already gone through years of continuous shame about not fitting in. Now he has to withstand the same feelings of vulnerability. Your challenge: Help him to recognize and enjoy his many successes—however they are defined—internal and external.

Gay men frequently have a hard time even knowing what they really look like. They may view themselves as less attractive than is the ideal (heavier, shorter, etc.), or in some other way have a distorted view. This warped perception undoubtedly translates into his striving endlessly for physical perfection, which is always elusive, and he then feels the relentless pain of not reaching the goal. This has old roots for many gay men. Body dissatisfaction is defined in literature as "Social Physique Anxiety." It is connected to internalized homophobia, and associated with a drive for masculinity. (Reilly, 2013; Brennan, 2012)

STEVEN:

Steven is a successful urban gay man. He has a sense of style and a nice wardrobe and has worked hard in therapy in order to feel proud of himself. He previously felt inadequate and didn't think that he measured up to the standards held by the Boston community in which he lives. Now that he has started online dating I wonder how he describes himself. When he responds that he sees himself as "nelly" and "girly," and then cannot think of anything else even when prodded, I am surprised.

Building on previous hypnosis imagery established by him, I continue pursuing his connection to nature, with the hope of eliciting more internal freedom. The words that spontaneously emerge to describe his feeling are, "Coming out of hibernation." A wonderful metaphor.

He explains, "When an animal comes out of hibernation, he wakes up slowly, wiggles his feet and toes, moves his legs, and thinks about staying put for a while longer. Because he is thirsty and needs to get up, he puts weight on his legs, moving to the front of the cave, and begins squinting at the sunlight as he brings himself out. After a long dormant cycle, he enjoys brightness. The animal is not extremely energetic, but able to get up and go out without wishing he did not have to." This depicts his quietness, depression, and social fears, as well as the moment of his moving forward.

Since he is coming out of his own hibernation and is ready to date, we explore issues about relationship and sex. Not only is seeing himself as nelly, a reflection of external standards within the gay community, there are internal barriers carried forward from his upbringing. In trance, he goes over the rules he has brought with him from his youth—rules that create limitations.

- You cannot be interested in more than one person at a time.
- You have to respond to someone if he interested in you, even if you don't feel interest.

- You have to put others before you.
- You make your bed and you lie in it. Suck it up.
- You constantly delay gratification.

In future sessions, I utilize his love of architecture to begin to carve out greater space. Once he leaves the cave, where will he be?

"I see two buildings—one that is old and dark. It is dull, depressed, overbearing and oppressive. It has libraries containing information on how to live a repressed and restrained life.

"Nearby is a newer building. It is sleek, and modern. This newer one monitors and connects to a database, with floor-to-ceiling windows. It is very bright and open, and people are sitting and reading monitors. I like it, but I don't know how to use anything."

This is important imagery, as he points to the discrepancy between the old ways from his past and the new ways that he likes but doesn't quite trust he can navigate. I am able to provide metaphorical and practical navigation tools as he takes further steps out of hibernation—leaving depression behind and looking forward to dating. He finishes this session with a hopeful image: "I am going to hang around in this new cool building and figure out how to work things out. I am determined. This is a good space for me."

THE GYM THE GYM THE GYM

You can't look good unless you spend a lot of time at the gym. That's the mantra. Indeed, it is a place to get into good shape and stay in good shape, but for gay men, it is also the place to be social. Many of your clients will make constant references to the interactions that take place there.

ONE REGULAR POUND EQUALS SEVEN GAY POUNDS

Feeling self-conscious or wishing to be slimmer and more muscular are common dilemmas for gay men. Here are a few provocative questions you can ask your client about their thoughts on the gym and their habits:

- Do you go for health reasons?
- Do you go for vanity?
- Do you go to be social?
- How do you feel inside if you miss a week?
- Do you fear your body will disintegrate?
- Do you over train and injure yourself?
- Does your adult gay body compensate for what you looked like or felt on the inside when you were growing up?

The answers to any or all of these questions will quickly reveal that despite how great gay men may look on the outside, they are relentlessly plagued by old fears on the inside. From Signorile, "No matter what we do, most of us will never become the masculine ideal we are striving for. But that doesn't stop us from trying." (Signorile, 1998, p. 8)

I had a weight trainer who often pointed to the unrealistic expectations of his clients. Your body type is your body type. Period. If you are tall and slim, you can't make your muscles look like a man who is stocky. If you are short and stocky, you can't be slim. Still, fantasy and determination make the gym the most popular place in town. Signorile defines what he calls "body fascism" as: "A rigid set of standards of physical beauty that pressures everyone to conform to them. Any person who doesn't meet this is deemed physically unattractive and sexually undesirable." (Signorile, 1998, p. 28)

Gay men are responding to the needs of other men, just as heterosexual women respond to the needs of men. They learn to sexualize themselves and to strive for a youthful appearance. These struggles around aging are enhanced by unrealistically comparing themselves to the images and beauty of younger men. Often, a 40, 50, 60, 70, or even 80- year-old gay man will come to my office describing how horrible he feels about himself. Self-acceptance, including one's appearance in accordance with one's chronological age, just doesn't come easy to a gay man.

The emphasis on youth in the gay male culture does a number on everyone. So-called accelerated aging refers to the truncated youth span among gay men. According to De Vries (2012): "Gay men are considered by self and others to be in midlife, or elderly, at earlier ages than heterosexual men." (Witten, 2012, p. 93)

THE SCENE AND THE UNSEEN

Signorile describes a man who doesn't meet the hot gay stereotype, yet feels a need to continue to go to the A-list events despite the rejection he experiences: "I want to feel I am completely involved in the scene. If I don't feel that I am at the center of the hippest people, of that 'in crowd,' of the sexiest and most A-list men, then I'll just feel worse." (Signorile, 1998, p. 23)

I sometimes wonder if overall gay men are honest with themselves regarding who they want to be and how they want to live. How many get caught in the urban net without questioning it? How many end up feeling trapped? In an effort to finally belong, what is given up?

Signorile describes the scene this way: "Scene refers to one predominantly white, middle class, and often upper-middle class segment of urban gay life that has significant cultural influence on much of the gay population." (Signorile, 1998, p. xxi) The pressure to be part of it is palpable, and yet it calls into question so many questions of core identity. My clients who are African American and Asian, for example, have frequently complained about being invisible and overlooked, and made fun of by white gay men. Unfortunately, gay men are as caught up in ignorance and bias as anyone else, despite having experienced this so directly themselves.

The so-called "in-crowd" is, of course, at the center of the scene. To be among rather than outside this crowd may be a driving force for many gay men, whether or not they are aware of it. This social scene may exclude heterosexuals and/or women. And while it may be seen as limiting on one level, on another, the forming of a close-knit group of friends is an important aspect of having community, particularly when family ties are not strong.

In my experience, the fantasy of perfection is related to early trauma. The unseen force at work: He needs to shed his past and does so by creating a beautiful facade. Many gay men who possess an impeccable eye use their talent to create something that is actually not real. Sometimes everything is so "perfect" in a home that it looks as though no one is really living there. This also can be true for a body or a wardrobe. The body is perfect, the wardrobe flawless, but no one seems to inhabit them. Gay men who have grown up in healthy, supportive families may exhibit similar interests—nice homes, bodies or wardrobes—but pursue them in a more casual and lighter way. What shines through is the real person. This subtler, more relaxed stance is strikingly different than someone whose life feels as though it depends on being perfect.

MARTIN:

Martin is about to turn 40. He is feeling badly about himself, as he compares himself to the idealized version of urban gay men. Some of the images are of men he knows and has crushes on, others are of men he has seen online. He is obsessed with the "A-list" gay men in Boston.

He also feels that 40 is over the hill and that the life he knows is going to fall away. (Of course, I am turning 50 and wish that I could be turning 40 all over again!)

In a burst of creativity I think of just the right script for him. The script's title, "Step into the Closet," is a bit ironic, since gay men have worked hard to be out of the closet. Notice how he confidently responds.

I ask him to imagine the closet of a successful gay man.

"I am looking inside the closet of a gay man who is around my age. There is a big walk-in closet, with eight Italian cut suits in shades of black, navy, and brown. Alongside the suits are nice long-sleeved dress shirts with interesting lines, colors, and patterns, and a wide assortment of shoes."

His face begins softening as it always does when he is in trance, and he begins to occupy the part of him that is relaxed, soft, and reassured. It is easy for me to assume he is describing his own closet.

"There is an antique bureau, and shelves toward the ceiling holding luggage, shoulder bags, and designer athletic clothes. These storage places hold the clothes that I enjoy. They give me different places to go—some casual, some showing off my physique—as well as the professional clothes I have. I can be daring in my variety of clothes.

"I see a full-length mirror. It is important to be able to look in the mirror and feel good about what I see."

It is exciting to hear him; he is owning the experience of being in a successful gay man's closet. I ask him to elaborate on the good things he sees, and the good feelings and emotions he is feeling inside of his body at that moment. He has a big smile on his face.

"You know what? I see a lot of my own clothes inside this closet. A lot of these things I already own—designer clothes, shoes, and bags. Wow, I fit in!"

Then I ask him to picture himself being in the gay neighborhood in the city, walking down the street, wearing his clothes, feeling a sense of pride and appreciating the ways in which he is perceived by others and how it feels.

"As I am walking down the streets, some people check me out. My head is up. I feel confident and strong."

Script: Step into the Closet

> *Step into the closet of a successful gay man. This closet might be a closet of a man your age, or someone older, or younger. Look around. What do you see? Describe the clothes that are there.* [Have him elaborate on clothes, shoes, luggage, how things are arranged, etc. Have him describe his sensory awareness of this.]
>
> *Try something on that you really like. Notice how you feel when you wear this. Notice how you look when you wear this.*

If you would like to, and whenever you feel ready, bring yourself outside onto a busy street, where you allow yourself to walk_with confidence. Really appreciate how it feels to be inside yourself, feeling confident and "fitting in." [Have him elaborate on what is happening.]

The success of this script comes from your own ability to help your client recognize that he can live in the present and feel good about how he lives as a gay man. For some, this means how they fit into the gay male community; for others it means accepting how they feel about their looks. The key is self-acceptance.

FACEBOOK AND SOCIAL MEDIA: GOOD-BYE REGIONAL, HELLO WORLDWIDE

With the rise of the internet, cultural differences have been replaced by global norms. The stereotypes of gay men are no longer regional. Today, pressures for being the perfect gay man are even more intense.

It is common that Facebook and other social media sites come up routinely in my sessions with clients. My gay clients often feel as though they fall short of the ideal man, based on who and what they see on online. Facebook promotes the illusion of having hundreds of "friends"—all fabulous, handsome, successful, worldly, and posting regularly. Thus, an enjoyable pastime easily slips into opportunities for old shame to rise up, and for that old friend, who is self-loathing, to show up again. Clients often feel they cannot compete with what they see, as they scroll through the postings of friends, friends of friends, and beyond.

Some provide links to sexy blogs, filled with iconic men in the gay community. World-renowned gay models, bartenders, porn stars, and handsome gay political figures —all who have large followings stare out of the screen waiting for the gay man to "like" him too. Signorile points out, "Porn stars are treated like royalty." (Signorile,

1998, p. 145)

Social media differs from print or television, based on the illusion of regular life. Posts are actually from real people who portray the perfect life of the urban gay male. Even the act of asking someone to be a "friend" feels a little like being in junior high school and readily accepting any morsel of attention from a popular peer. Additionally, with the links available to other blogs and availability of other social media sites, internet addiction is on the rise, as the quality of life and experiences of mindfulness and meaning diminishes. We need to continually reinforce the significance of unplugging and taking time for self. Experiential work is received fully because so many are lacking any positive sense of meaning.

GAY MEN LIVING OUTSIDE THE CITY

So, the gay male stereotype doesn't affect those who live in a rural setting. Right? They are living happy lives in the country; perhaps they are older and in a relationship. Not true. Yes, many gay men live more peaceful existences away from the pressure and chaos of the urban gay male world. However, I assure you that these men also feel the pressures described. Whether it's online media or magazines, television, film or advertising, the gay man living in the country is bombarded by the same powerful images that tell him what he should or could be. Images of the urban gay paragon reach beyond the city limits. Similarly, most women—urban, suburban, and rural—are affected by the media stereotype of the young, thin, beautiful woman. Even if she accepts herself as she is, chances are that when she catches her reflection unexpectedly or flips though a copy of *Vogue*, she feels the queasiness of that internal comparison.

If our gay male clients are navigating the complexities of living the dream life, as therapists, we need to help them:

- Truly understand how the tendency to look perfect can be destructive.

- Strike a balance between appearance and appreciating what matters most on an essential level.
- Become empowered to celebrate their most authentic self, based on inherent strengths.
- Make realistic decisions about appearance based on the truth of what they look like.
- Shift away from comparing themselves to others, toward seeing themselves as the real meaningful marker.

CHAPTER SIX
Speaking of Sex

SO, LET'S TALK ABOUT SEX

As I started to write this important chapter, I was worried...about being too general or too specific, about being a spokesperson for gay sex, about exposing my personal life. I was just worried. And it wasn't lost on me that my nervousness was in line with the instinct to hide—something that is common to all gay men.

Not surprisingly, I always feel just a little awkward bringing up the topic of sex in therapy sessions. How will clients react? Will I provide enough of what they want and need to feel safe?

This discomfort is even more intense when I am working with a population to which I do not belong—heterosexuals, for instance. So, yes, if you are not a gay male therapist, you can assume that sex will be a challenging aspect of the therapeutic conversation. As Dr. Polonsky points out, "Your clients will feel awkward, you may want to make it comfortable, yet most likely, neither one of you will. There is no way NOT to feel uncomfortable." (Polonsky, 2012, p. 1) When working with gay men, there are some central questions to ask yourself that will help preempt moments of even greater awkwardness. These things are going to come up!

Some Questions To Ask Yourself:

- What are your internal instinctual reactions toward gay men?
- Will you seem comfortable when discussing sex with your client?
- How do you feel about discussing masturbation?
- Will you find the right words?
- Are you certain that what you are saying is accurate?
- Will you worry about offending him?
- Do you have any thoughts about people having anal intercourse?
- Are you prudish according to gay male standards? Do you worry that this will show?
- Do you worry that your own sexual proclivities will somehow be revealed to your client?
- How do you feel about open relationships?
- How do you feel about internet pornography?
- How do you feel about people who have HIV or STDs, as a result of anonymous sex?

DEVELOPING EASE WITH DISCOMFORT

Years ago, one of my heterosexual colleagues said, "I don't have any trouble imagining gay men being sexual together, but I can't imagine them on a dance floor dancing together." This is something I have often thought about. If she couldn't picture two men dancing together, how could she possibly feel comfortable with them being sexual together? I laughed politely, but inside I was experiencing an old familiar feeling that I knew all to well: a combination of shame, self-consciousness, and a desire to gently redirect the conversation to something else.

Even if you are comfortable, remember that your client has learned how to protect himself when interacting with authority figures. Revealing his sexual practices is one of the most vulnerable experiences he may have in his therapy with you.

Hearing about a client's escapades, the frequency of his sexual encounters, the risks he is taking with unsafe sex or his cheating on his partner, are just some of the things that may be part of the conversation in sessions. Increasing your own ability to deal with these issues, both internally and externally, is crucial.

All therapists at some point will have to address several of these topics with clients, whether or not the clients are gay. Of course, you could steer clear of the general subject altogether, or you could keep finding reasons to put the discussion off. But, as Hedges makes clear: "The answer is not to avoid or back off from meaningful relating, but rather to step up to relationships and work hard toward achieving this." (Hedges, 2011, p.168)

WHAT IS NORMAL?

The question of normalcy is loaded. Gay male sexuality is varied and complicated. A gay man may develop a comfortable acceptance of his sexuality and enjoy this freedom, receiving reinforcement from the gay male community. Or, perhaps he is actually ignoring the unhealthy aspects of his behaviors. What is considered normal in the gay male community can sometimes support unhealthy aspects of sexuality, including denial. It is common for gay men to compartmentalize their behaviors, which mitigates the chances for an honest assessment of sexual practices.

My postulation is that compared to heterosexuals gay men are freer in the sexual domain. Author and psychotherapist Robert Weiss also shares this belief. "His increasingly destructive patterns of sexual behavior take place against a cultural background of dramatically greater sexual freedoms than those enjoyed by his heterosexual peers." (Weiss, 2005, p. 65)

Sex is widely accessible to gay men. Anonymous sex has its roots in earlier times when married men assumed to be heterosexual would go out cruising for anonymous sexual encounters with other men in parks or rest areas.

Some heterosexual men might wish that they could be as sexually free as gay men, but the norms are different. For those who are comfortable talking about sex with their gay friends, the common response is one of envy.

There are also men who experience fear due to the openness of sexuality in the gay male community. It may be that internalized homophobia, unresolved feelings about being gay, or ongoing trauma issues sustain this fear. Some of my clients avoid dealing with these potential feelings by not engaging in sex at all. Unfortunately, that choice usually leads to one's self-esteem and confidence becoming eroded over time.

BRAD:

In his ongoing hypnosis work, we explore how Brad accommodates other men, leaving his own needs aside. This theme touches most every aspect of Brad's life.

He comes up with some helpful new insights in trance:

"Sexually, I felt that I must keep giving, be available at all moments, and never have control over what I want for myself, abuse history number 355!"

"I am following an old strategy that is not serving me well anymore. From now on I will discuss who I am, and what I want as I begin dating and being sexual. It has been a dream to present myself as I truly am, unedited. I want to be with a man who loves me for this."

WHAT SEX IS, VERSUS WHAT IT SHOULD BE

I can explain why gay men have internalized expectations about what their sex lives should be: the affliction of stereotypes. For many people, sex means intercourse. Anything that isn't intercourse doesn't count. This is sometimes the case with gay men as well. If you use the word "sex" with your clients, you need to be very specific about what you mean. When you question a gay man about his sex life, he may be obtuse, minimizing anonymous encounters with men he meets online or in public cruising places. These encounters "don't count."

A quick example: Michael had cheated on his long-time partner and decided it was important to confess the truth to him, but only the partial truth. He decided that if he shared his infidelities had taken place in a steam room, his partner wouldn't be bothered. I reminded him that what was relevant were the specific sexual behaviors he had engaged in, rather than the locations of where they took place. Michael and I laughed about the distortion in which gay men often find comfort: It is more acceptable for a gay male to cheat in a steam room than somewhere else. The random, quick, anonymous setting of the interaction seems to be a norm gay with which men are okay.

Polonsky (Polonsky "It's not only about sex," p. 2) describes internalized cultural norms, for which he uses the phrase, "obligatory protocol." An obligatory protocol for gay men is related to anal sex. One man is a top, the other is a bottom, and all gay men are supposed to enjoy it. "Are you a top or are you a bottom?" This is the question that precedes many sexual encounters, reinforcing that anal sex is the only way to go, and that most men have one position or the other. Further, the stereotype also connects the bottom position to passivity and the top to dominance.

Just recently, a client was concerned that as a top, he was too passive, since all tops are supposed to be assertive. I suggested that a top can be passive, and that rigid roles need not hold true for everyone. The next day, clients in my therapy group were discussing how societal acceptance of gay men has resulted in more freedom so that traditional sex roles weren't as important as they used to be.

Gay men are as complex as anyone else, with diverse feelings and desires. In the privacy of my psychotherapy office, many clients discuss feeling deficient or peculiar because they don't like anal sex. As a result, erectile dysfunctions are common, but kept secret. However, this is something that cannot be hidden from a sexual partner.

Of course, many gay men enjoy anal sex, but some are versatile, whereas other men have satisfying sexual lives with oral sex, or mutual masturbation, or masturbation.

The truth is that sexual compatibility occurs on a multitude of levels. The experience of physical attraction in and of itself can be a wonderful and satisfying connection between two people, regardless of specific sexual acts. Sometimes people are so busy looking for sexual compatibility preferences they miss the other nuanced connections that exist between them.

HYPNOSIS: A KEY TO BEFRIENDING THE BODY

Access to the full spectrum of sexual expression is in part dependent on a friendly connection to one's body. As I discussed earlier, gay men have been betrayed by their bodies. Experiential work can help them befriend their bodies. Building on your good connection, hypnosis can be employed to encourage clients to reclaim the safety and care of their bodies. Relaxation is a simple, straightforward, and powerful way to guide gay men to experience great pleasure in the most basic of ways. This work can be done slowly and gently, nothing fancy. Teaching gay male clients how to feel comfortable, and how to be patient and relaxed, can be central to their growth in this area. If the body moves from being a conflicted place fraught with anxiety, to being a place of rest and enjoyment, the positive impact on self-image and relationship will be immeasurable.

After a time, you can add more depth to the experience by incorporating metaphors regarding strength, or moving forward steadily and with confidence.

LEIGH:

Leigh was initially referred for hypnotherapy because of difficulties getting and maintaining erections. Ironically, he would wake up in the middle of the night fully erect and could not understand why this was happening since he wasn't able to get an erection during the day.

He has been with his partner for years and reports that they have a good sexual relationship. He uses Viagra and injections in order to get erections. Though he has a history of depression, symptoms are no longer prominent. During the course of treatment it becomes clear that he has a history of trauma as well.

I decide that the best place to start is by using the Secure Place script (Chapter Two). I ask him to imagine a place where he feels protected and describe what he experiences:

"I am struck by how relaxed I feel. I usually feel a block between my groin and my chest. I want to do more work on opening up my chest. Often I am closed up really tightly. It is armor and a protection that serves me well and I have been afraid to let go of it. I instantaneously pictured a down comforter pulled over my shoulders, which feels very warm and protective. Wow! I feel like crying, but I don't need to anymore because I now can push the sadness away with this safe place."

Over the next several sessions, we continue to do hypnosis. We focus on comfort and confidence. I take my time during the beginning of these inductions, slowly leading him into hypnosis. I emphasize my own feelings of confidence in the benefits of hypnosis, in sharing the power of incorporating the experience of bringing the mind and body together by doing this work, and in his own abilities to succeed. I do this by using strength and optimism in the tone of my voice, as well confident words that encourage him to trust the process, trust me, and most important, trust his body. This takes confidence on my end, to gently lead him, while modeling comfort and assertiveness and implying safety with boundaries, something of which he is not accustomed. I sense this is necessary in order to help him work on his sexuality. At times, it felt as though this approach was all that was needed throughout his sessions.

After a few sessions, I ask him to imagine something opening with a zipper. It serves as a wonderful metaphor for being more open sexually. I am taking a bit of a chance, but it works just I hoped. I feel comfortable, knowing that his positive and self-focused previous experiences in trance provided him with the powerful opening in his chest—something for which he had been looking.

The next week he exclaims, "I am feeling lighter and more excitable now. I feel more positive. The pipes are no longer clogged!"

How thrilling. As we do more hypnosis he says, "I feel like I am on a tricycle. You are in back of me, supporting me. I am playing in child-like glory! The dark feelings in my stomach are breaking up and I am allowing myself to embrace feelings; allowing myself to be happy. I like this space. It is so good!"

It is clear to me that the combination of enjoying hypnosis and the positive connection and safety of our relationship is helping him to break away from the confines of his usual existence.

In subsequent hypnosis sessions we explore his sexuality and his sensuality on a deeper level. He visualizes being at home and exploring his body. "I am laughing and smiling. I am enjoying myself. I look at myself in the bathroom mirror and I see myself as a strong, powerful, and sexy man. I am embracing my age, and the imperfections with my body tell a wonderful story. This has always been a battle and maybe I have never liked or wanted to look at my body until now. The flaws that exist are good and they are sexy."

This is significant for someone who has never come to terms with his trauma history or trusted in his sexuality. True self-acceptance in the face of so many overwhelming images of the gay male ideal is impressive.

During these sessions, while exploring memories of sex in his teenage years and reliving them in trance, I continue to use statements that affirm his sexuality and being gay. It is delightful to see him responding positively to his own sexuality.

"I am liking myself! I am taking the time to enjoy my body inside and out, and realize just how many times I used to automatically demean myself. Now I feel good just being me." As he continues, a faint smile comes over his face. "I see an image of cracking the shell. Brown glass shatters and I am breaking it and peeling it off. Underneath is a younger layer of soft, white, healthy and fresh skin. The light is back."

He is smiling with a child-like grin on his face, and says, "Feeling bad allowed me to define my sexual being in a way that was not accurate. It is time to let go of the pain. I can slowly watch it go on its way. I constantly felt guilty for being sexual. Now I realize I don't need to anymore. My light has just changed. Full steam ahead!"

After working with Leigh in hypnosis, I am even more certain that the combination of hypnosis in psychotherapy yields significant and powerful results.

WHEN EVERYTHING IS POSSIBLE IS ANYTHING PROBABLE?

With all of the ways to meet or hook up with other people these days, how we find partners has changed dramatically, even from just a generation ago. This is as true for gay men as for everyone else—and maybe a bit more. The internet provides many alluring opportunities. So-called social sites offer galleries of tantalizing pictures, including pornographic photos on smart phone apps. There are services available that let viewers know the locations of other interested men. Texts and more pictures can be forwarded instantly. You describe what you are looking for and the service tells you where you can find it right then. It is quick, random, and easy. However, the fun doesn't come free of charge.

The actual Mr. Right becomes more and more elusive as the fantasy Mr. Right—sometimes dozens of fantasy Mr. Rights—pop up every time you click Enter. The search quickly becomes addictive. Thanks to the ease of the internet, Mr. Right may live anywhere in the world, or nowhere in the real world. The use of portable devices can easily become compulsive. Add to this the lure of having a live man respond, and the digital world can be endlessly stimulating and confusing. Since flirtation, vagueness, or deception are often the norm, the state of arousal remains constant and can be stirred up in a moment's notice. Since visiting these sites is considered normal among gay men, the compulsive nature of the sites isn't even questioned.

Another distressing phenomenon related to social media is that gay men don't even need to leave their homes to find that for which they are looking. Why bother to get out of your pajamas or even shower when the quest for a man is browser based, and just a click away?

These ideas are so entrenched that many gay men (and others) just assume that this is the way to go about meeting others and they miss out on real possibilities as they sequester themselves inside with their sleek machines. Many of my clients sheepishly confess to being online several hours a day, simultaneously surfing various sites. Even when they are away from their computers or phone, they keep their status as "logged on."

Some joke that in gay resort towns, such as Provincetown where I live, you used to see men strolling along the streets to engage with others, but because many are now doing this at home the exciting energy on the streets has diminished. I am not sure how accurate this is, but those who are plugged in are indeed missing out on good old-fashioned connections and the unmistakable chemistry that happens in certain real-life encounters.

THE DANGERS OF DON'T ASK DON'T TELL

Recently, a gay client asked me for a referral to a gay male physician. He was sexually active, and due to embarrassment, hadn't told his older heterosexual doctor, even though his doctor might have felt perfectly fine with this information. I found the client a gay male physician so that he would be able to talk more explicitly about his sexual adventures, and his concerns.

If you are a heterosexual therapist, it is even more difficult for your clients to discuss sex with you. They may be particularly guarded and private about their sex lives. If they are engaging in behaviors that they assume you won't understand or approve of, they will be silent. Often, I hear from gay males that they don't want to be the ones who have to educate their therapists about gay sex.

Hedges comments "Sexually sensitive interactions from psychotherapeutic work have seldom been reported in our literature, or in a courageous manner." (Hedges, 2011, p. 77) The point is, that it is up to us to provide and encourage comfort. If you don't ask your patients about their sexual practices, they are not going to volunteer the information. Finding ways to talk about sex is tough, yet crucial for success in therapy. Taking a sexual history with people is very important, yet it is often not done.

NOT SPEAKING OF SEX...

There are many reasons why practitioners avoid talking about sex, whether it is that they don't have proper training for it, or that they are reluctant to ask direct questions for fear of being too intrusive. When the gender or sexual preference of the client is different, there is a concern that it may be inappropriate or not politically correct to ask questions. Polonsky observes: "Unless your client's presenting problem is specifically sexual, do not assume that he will bring up anything sexual unless you ask about it directly." (Polonsky, 2011, p. 17)

HOW TO INITIATE A DISCUSSION

Polonsky teaches about the importance of addressing sexual issues, not only as they manifest in the present, and but as they emerged in adolescence when clients are likely to first become sexually active. (Polonsky, 2011) The latter area of discussion may reveal issues pertaining to being gay that you wouldn't have known otherwise.

Polonsky points out that all teens experience discomfort with their emerging sexuality. (Polonsky, 2011) As teens, most gays were secretive, filled with shame, took risks to find sexual partners, and inevitably were exposed, made fun of, or abused, based on their sexual interests. One doesn't walk away from these experiences without being scarred. By the time adults seek help for their sexual difficulties, they have internalized a self that has been colored by years of feeling incompetent, afraid, and ashamed.

When it comes to sexual development, boys frequently have to fend for themselves, with little respectful guidance from adults. The mechanics of sex, the problems encountered, how to manage them, and the emotions generated are not topics that are addressed. Where gay men got their early sexual information, and where they still do, is important to know. This provides a key to treatment. Often, gay men are misinformed through the media. Frequently, distorted images and stereotypes are fully absorbed without question, and old twisted pieces of information, acquired from dubious sources when they were young, have never been updated.

BLAKE:

Blake decided to see me for psychotherapy after years of seeing a heterosexual male therapist. He questioned his own ability to discuss sex openly with the previous therapist. He feels very conflicted about leaving this therapist about whom he cares deeply.

It takes Blake a few sessions to begin talking about sex, even though this is the issue he presents. Despite being aware of my comfort, he needs to go slowly. I honor his carefulness and move at his pace. As the details of his sexual experiences unfold, I decide to ask him about his teenage sexual years. This opens up a depth of richness. Blake shares complex stories that intertwine his coming out with his mother's disapproval of the gay pornography she finds in his room. In a desire to please his mother, he put his sexual energy on hold for years. He became secretive about his interests and activities, and this behavior, established in his teens, continues into the present. In fact, the theme of secrecy is now intertwined with what excites him sexually. Concealing himself is preferred to true intimacy.

Furthermore, I connected how instead of confronting the issue, secrecy had contributed to him leaving his former therapist and switching to me. I am curious how he will handle differences with me over time. My intention is to encourage openness and assertive communication, while accepting that he can be loved and satisfied simultaneously. I will work this into our discussions to reinforce its importance, even when we aren't talking about sex.

QUESTIONS TO ASK CLIENTS

Since it is not often that clients will initiate any discussion of sex, it is up to you to begin this process. Polonsky (2012) suggests the following questions:

- I am curious to learn more about how you acquired information about sex.Do you have any difficulty getting or maintaining an erection?
- Do you go on any websites that are sexual, and if so, which ones?

He also describes the "third person invisible," which is a way to ask sensitive questions by framing them in the third person (Polonsky, 2012). This format helps to lessen defensiveness: "Some people complain of...Has this ever happened for you?"

This approach is normalizing and less intimidating than direct methods. People are more apt to answer with less self-consciousness and greater honesty. In general, using normalizing statements can put people at ease, and when it comes to sexuality, especially in trance, they will help take the charge and embarrassment out of the conversation.

Questions I Ask My Clients:

- How did your family discuss or avoid discussion of sex?
- How did you discover pornography? How did you get gay pornography—and at what age?
- Were you ever caught masturbating? How was that handled?
- Were you ever caught having sex with guy friends? How was that handled? How did you feel at the time?

From these questions, a host of issues may come to the surface, including smaller or more significant traumas, acceptance or lack of it around being gay, wounds to self-esteem, and more. Clients tend to answer in rich detail and pertinent therapy topics will automatically present themselves.

ONE MORE THING

Often, clients prefer to generalize their answers when discussing their sexual habits, especially while describing the ways in which they meet other gay men. "The internet" is a vague answer that is both an answer and a catchall, which keeps them from having to elaborate or exposing their true selves.. Many of us will simply nod yes, without asking more. Again, the richness of relevant details will direct your work. So, a nudge toward specificity:

- Which phone apps do you use?
- Which websites do you visit?

With these questions, you imply that they will answer directly, not vaguely. You won't be surprised to find out that they are on four or five different websites where they are looking for sex, including various phone apps, which they have running simultaneously. If you aren't specific with your questions, you won't get the answers that will ultimately be beneficial to them.

Think about it: You are working with a person with a drinking problem and you ask, "Did you drink too much?" The answer may come back, "No." That doesn't tell you much. If you ask, "How many drinks do you have per night?" rather than "How many times a week do you drink?" the answer will be more specific. If you ask about the size of the glass being used, you are going to receive information that is even more specific. As your clients sense your comfort in asking relevant questions, they will respond more openly.

BELOW THE BELT

The exact words you use while discussing sex should match your client's style. How people talk about sex is revealing, and by paying attention to their language and style you will discover how best to communicate with them. Once I have convinced my clients that it is okay to talk about sex, especially in the context of their individual therapy, I mentally note the words they use. Some keep it formal, with clinical or medical terms, while others talk as if they are describing a pornographic scene from a movie. Enlisting their tone and even word choice is one way to employ Ericksonian concepts of utilization and tailoring. With one client it may be most appropriate to use the word "penis," whereas with another the word "dick" might be used, or perhaps "cock." Being flexible is intrinsic to utilization and tailoring.

Remember the sacred therapeutic relationship. Hedges reassures his clients about sharing details regarding sexuality by reinforcing the importance and uniqueness of this relationship: "We talk all we want about anything, and it is rather nice that we have this boundary to keep us safe." (Hedges, 2011, p. 73)

This is the place where your approval begins to compensate for a client's previous painful experiences of being gay, especially concerning their sexual history. Your caring is infectious.

Sometimes a little nudge from me helps my clients to open up more. I frequently remind them of my experience as a therapist: "You know what? As I sit in this chair, I hear these kinds of experiences all day long. Since you are sitting over there, of course it is much harder for you than it is for me. I am totally comfortable hearing and talking about sex if/or when you feel ready to discuss it." This type of reflection emphasizes both my comfort and my experience, and in response clients often will take the risk of speaking openly.

In another circumstance I might say, "You seem a little uncomfortable. I can't tell if you're uncomfortable about talking of sex in general, or if you're worried about how I'll react. I can assure you that I'm completely comfortable—I talk about this stuff all day long."

In addition, it is helpful to have consultations with therapists/colleagues who can assist you to intervene more effectively. Admitting vulnerabilities will steer us in the right direction: to reach out for suggestions and guidance to help, you help your clients feel understood in the treatment relationship. You can also find a great deal of information about gay sex and sexually transmitted diseases from urban LGBTQ community health centers, as well as public health departments.

ARE ALL GAY RELATIONSHIPS OPEN?

Open relationships—relationships that are non-monogamous—are not uncommon in the gay male community. Like many other modes of sexuality in the gay community, this model is easily accepted, without people assessing whether it suits their needs, or whether their relationship has the strength to sustain the pattern. Over the years I have heard many of my clients say that all gay men cheat on their partners. This simply is not true. Those who don't believe monogamous relationships work may have bought into this stereotype without questioning it or looking deeper. There are many couples that maintain monogamy, based on their choosing and their needs. Perhaps they feel less comfortable discussing this openly if it isn't viewed as the norm. Or perhaps they simply prefer privacy!

Monogamy and non-monogamy are options for gay couples. Unlike in the mainstream heterosexual community, the latter option does not carry a stigma. This choice reflects a liberal stance regarding gay sexuality in comparison to the general population. Sometimes this can be positive, but sometimes it encourages freedom even when people are not comfortable with it.

Unfortunately, many couples don't assess the strength of their relationship before making the decision to switch to an open relationship. Or many switch during problematic times, which is a recipe for disaster. Making this transition isn't the way to ameliorate relational or communication problems. Opening up a relationship is challenging and rocky. Some decide to pursue an open relationship in order to avoid confronting the challenging problems that exist in the relationship. But this decision never strengthens a vulnerable relationship; it can only really work if the relationship is already strong.

Frankly, this is a tricky topic for most therapists. Aside from practice, there is no easy way to gain comfort with the topic. Speak to client. If you have no gay clients, speak to colleagues. Get educated. You will develop a sense of ease over time. Questions around monogamous and open relationships are relevant for all gay men, single or partnered.

ATTACHMENT AND SEXUALITY

DAN:

Dan had been in Sex and Love Addicts Anonymous for two years when he began treatment with me. Aside from numerous random hookups, he had also been arrested for public sex.

Around sixth grade, he started being sexual with a friend whom he "serviced." There was no reciprocity but Dan remembers loving him. He was more than happy to be needed since his parents were unavailable. He described feeling safe and secure with this friend. It lasted for about three years until they were caught. The relationship abruptly ended. Dan never fully recovered from the painful loss.

As he describes these details to me, I think about whether the origins of Dan's sexual addiction are related to his unmet attachment needs; his need to be needed keeps him in the cycle of compulsive behaviors.

LOOKING FOR CONNECTION

A common theme for gay men is to use sex as a vehicle for finding intimacy and love. I speak to my clients about whether they are really looking for a long-term relationship (paying attention to how they meet men), and what they would like as the outcome. Looking for an intimate relationship is not the same thing as using sex apps that are designed for hooking up with guys nearby, or going to a bathhouse or a cruising spot. The intention and energy is very different. Many gay men don't agree with me on this and I have had several conversations about this with my clients over the years. The important questions are: When is sex just sex? and When is sex related to attachment issues? Gay men use sex to meet their emotional needs.

Hedges described one man: "While Tom seeks connection through sexual stimulation, at some level he also knows how to use sexuality to avoid, or to rupture possible connections." (Hedges, 2011, p. 70)The description alludes to a dismissive attachment style. Hedges elaborates even further to portray the psychodynamic reasons that people pursue sex for attachment and points out that the search for security and love is a desire to replicate the primary bonding pattern that the infant and toddler experienced with caregivers. (Hedges, 2011)

Each person learns how to relate and form intimacy with others, based on his or her own unique attachment style. This is so for both sexual partners. Sometimes individual needs intersect simultaneously to provide a sexually and emotionally satisfying outcome, while other times each person has his or her own distinct needs, leading to complicated outcomes based on different expectations.

Corbett writes about this. "I thought as well about the ways in which his temporary attachments to the men he described might enact the ambivalence inherent in a paternal internalization, a simultaneous quest for attachment to, identification with, and rejection of these men. I thought about how few usable paternal, parental figures there had been in his life." (Corbett, 2009, p. 227)

THREE ATTACHMENT STYLES

There are three main attachment styles: secure, insecure (or anxious), and dismissive. An understanding of these styles is relevant in understanding sex in the gay male community.

Secure Attachment

People with a secure attachment style can have truly intimate connections with significant others. They are capable of being available, responsive, and are able to view others similarly. The securely attached person is able to experience a true sense of security and intimacy and knows that this can be attainable for himself. His partners are experienced as trustworthy and reliable, and he is capable of a long, stable, satisfying relationship. (Birnbaum, 2006)Many long-term gay relationships consist of two men who are secure in their attachment styles, despite norms in the gay community that might challenge security.

Not every long-term partnership consists of two securely attached men. Many men find their way to each other and find a way to stay together, despite each having unhealthy attachment issues. Securely attached couples, however, tend to stay together for the right reasons.

In addition, a sexually active gay male with a secure attachment is able to discern who is a good sexual match for him. He can sense safety, danger, and even opt out of circumstances that he knows may not be healthy for him. For example, he may avoid hooking up with people who are overly needy and looking for more than he wants to give. This is a healthy level of discernment and self-respect. Of course, most people make mistakes and have regrets about certain sexual experiences.

HEALTHY ATTACHMENT TRAITS AND GAY MALE SEXUALITY

Before Sex:

- He can distinguish between his needs for sex and intimacy, and make choices that allow him to feel in control.
- He can experience safety and intimacy and enjoy these possibilities.
- He can sense danger and opt out of meeting or hooking up, if that is what's best for him.

During Sex:

- He can enjoy sex for what it is with his partner, without attributing more to it than there is.
- He can feel present, relaxed, and connected during sex.
- He has a sense of self and can comfortably assert his likes and dislikes.

- He has the ability to say no to those people or situations in which he isn't comfortable.

After Sex:

- He can appreciate intimacy that stems from sex, and pursue it further afterward, but with a sense of security.
- He can learn from mistakes and can account for them as he shapes his behaviors in the future.
- He will utilize support if he needs to sort more out for himself.
- He can remove himself from psychological danger by staying away from those who are not good for him.

Dismissive Attachment

A dismissive attachment style is defined as the person who emotionally distances himself from relationships and partners as his default behavior. He strives for self-reliance at all costs. He has learned that others are untrustworthy and disappointing. As a result, his privacy and ability to remain concealed come first. Communication styles are typically curt, evasive, and unemotional, since the unstated purpose in interactions is to avoid emotional connection, intimacy, or dependence on another person.

Dismissive people avoid intimate connections with others, and whether or not they are aware of it, they distrust others' good will, or a partner's good intentions. This is called a dismissive "deactivation strategy." (Birnbaum, 2006) A dismissive gay man is less likely to fall in love, or to allow himself to fall in love, or to be in long-term relationships. He dismisses motives that promote closeness and he exerts manipulation and control in order to protect himself. He finds a way to emotionally disconnect while involved in sexual activity so that he can partake in sex without allowing himself to experience true, intimate feelings. He is apt to engage in anonymous sex, since one-time sexual encounters with strangers are easier, because there is a lack of emotional connectedness.

Men tend to adopt a more recreational orientation toward sexuality than women, and emphasize the expression of sexual needs. They are motivated by and emphasize physical release. Factor this in for a gay man with a dismissive attachment style and though he may be perceived as sexy, he indeed will be inaccessible to his partners.

The norms of gay male sex can be perceived as dismissive, due to what is deemed typical in the gay community. Anonymous and recreational encounters that do not involve any kind of emotional connection are common. Even when clients convince themselves that they are seeking intimacy, where and how they are seeking connection (online, phone apps, sex clubs, anonymous encounters, etc.) may be a way of sustaining this dismissive stance without even realizing it.

If you are evaluating your client's sexuality and you aren't gay, this is important to keep in mind, especially because of the prevalence of casual gay male sex. Gay men simply assume that the norms regarding sexuality in their culture are perfectly healthy. If you are not gay, your client may assume that you will not understand. If you are gay, your client may expect you to automatically assume a similar posture without challenging him, which is often what my clients expect from me.

DISMISSIVE TRAITS AND GAY MALE SEXUALITY

Before sex:

- As he is looking for sex, he will most likely be evasive, and give very little of his true self.
- He may be perceived by others as masculine and mysterious, which can be quite a turn-on.
- If he is really good looking, his stereotypical masculine stance will evoke projection from potential conquests, which can lead to anger or rejection from those who seek him out.
- He will shy away from clingy types, which will only reinforce clinginess in certain others.

During sex:

- He will perform in a perfunctory way and avoid intimacy, such as eye contact, cuddling, and holding.

- He will have his technique "down cold," as he has learned to perfect his way of connecting without connecting.
- If he has a trauma history, or the current partner has a trauma history, certain intimacies can be easily activated so that he will maintain an even greater distance.

After sex:

- He will be quick to leave.
- He needs to avoid intimacy and most likely will have somewhere he needs to be in order to escape.
- It may appear as though he had just acted a role in a performance that ends abruptly, rather than participating in a meaningful encounter.

Dismissive men may be perceived as narcissistic. An interesting observation is that this is a typical archetype of masculinity in the gay community: ultra-masculine and ultra-cool. Yet, someone who appears so appealing can actually be emotionally harmful to many.

Anxious or Insecure Attachment

An anxious attachment includes a pattern in which the person perceives other people as insufficiently available to provide support and protection. Because of his history, this type of gay man worries that others won't be there in times of need. As a result, he imagines, creates, or manipulates scenarios to secure availability. This isn't done purposely, or for that matter, even consciously. His attachment style is so ingrained, that insecurity is all he knows, and it drives him to unhealthy scenarios, over and over again.

Vacillation is common. Imagine if you have an overly anxious client who is constantly attempting to win the love and approval of others, sexual or otherwise. It is often perceived as a turn-off, especially for those who value privacy or possess dismissive traits. When your client is in a sexual situation, he may try to win the love and approval of others, whether it is a partner or a complete stranger, and he will most likely go overboard with neediness. He will easily feel slighted and actually create encounters in which he feels rejected or does not understand what happened. This may likely evoke frustration in you.

A person with anxious attachment (or insecure attachment) invests in holding and caressing, as opposed to more sexual behavior. He just cannot get his needs met. He is likely to focus on satisfying his partner while putting his own needs aside. He can be obsessive, clingy, and exhibit controlling behaviors. In his need for connection, he makes sure that those he is involved with play by his rules. He may vacillate between being insecure and having temper tantrums. This is because attachment anxiety amplifies the effects of positive and negative sexual experiences and relationship interactions. (Birnbaum, 2006) A person with an anxious attachment pursues sexual activities in an attempt to fulfill unmet emotional needs, such as security and love. As a result, sex is not about sex. Someone who feels unloved uses sexual activities to fill himself emotionally. He may have a difficult time deciphering which partner will be good for him.

Additionally, gay men with insecure attachment behavior will likely put themselves in risky sexual situations. They may engage in unsafe sex in an attempt to satisfy emotional emptiness. even though they are well aware of the physical risks, Feeling accepted and loved wins out, even over the possibility of developing HIV or other sexually transmitted diseases. Education, of course, is important, but being educated doesn't guarantee that people are going to adhere to safer sex guidelines.

INSECURE ATTACHMENT TRAITS AND GAY MALE SEXUALITY

Before sex:

- He will be overly eager to hook up and make a connection.
- He will overlook any warning signs or red flags, and proceed without caution. The goal is to make the connection, even if it isn't attainable.

- He will look for validation externally.
- He will promise sexual acts for the sake of acceptance that put him at risk of diseases.

During sex:

- He will do whatever he can to turn a sexual encounter into an emotional connection.
- He will find a way to fool himself by creating a mood or environment that is romantic.
- He will have unsafe sex in order to feel accepted or loved.
- He will disregard his own needs to win over his partner, yet feel rejected.

After sex:

- He will want to cuddle and cherish time spent together. He will do whatever is needed to accommodate his partner, even if it was just a hookup.
- He may initially feel satisfied that his needs are met, but will soon find himself wanting more.
- He will experience disappointment and feel rejected by those whose motives are different from his own. (This happens repeatedly.)

A basic understanding of these attachment traits will be helpful as you work with gay male clients. As a therapist you need to expand your sense of why your clients may be driven to pursue sexual activities in ways that they do—ways that may be hard to understand logically—but make clear what the drive may be about.

Therapeutic intervention rooted in compassion, knowledge, and broad understanding will be more effective than intervention that is dogmatic, overly authoritative, and shame-based. Further, your interventions will be less authoritative and shame-based. Recognizing the deeper emotional components of sexual engagement is essential to efficacious therapy with gay men.

CHAPTER SEVEN
When Sex Is a Problem

Gay men have often learned to dissociate from their bodies. The prohibition against gay sex, against being gay, period, creates a highly conflicted relationship between a man and his body beginning at a very early age.

Compartmentalization is apt to be strongest in the sexual realm, since this is the place where shame has been felt the most during upbringing. As I previously mentioned, gay men are quick to assume that a norm in their community is acceptable without even questioning its impact. Therefore, sexual compulsivity and addiction are prominent in the gay male community.

As a therapist, how do you decide if a client's sexual behavior is healthy within the norms of the gay community, or whether his behavior is compulsive? If you are not a gay therapist, you may think that his behaviors are compulsive. If you are a gay therapist, you may not. Neither perspective is ever going to be entirely right across the board. This is confusing for everyone.

MICHAEL:

Michael isolates himself from other gay men. He justifies his masturbation and porn addiction. He buys gay porn and has such an extensive collection that he hasn't even looked at a fraction of what he has purchased. He spends hours on end watching movies and masturbating.

We decide to use hypnosis to explore why his pornography addiction continues to get worse. After starting with a basic trance, here is what he says:

"Pornography gives me independence. Everyone but me is having sex or having children, so pornography is my partner and my sexual release. When I am in my room with the door shut, I feel better. Since there is no excitement in my life, I have the excitement of buying movies. I know when I am going over my budget and it feels dangerous, and since I have screwed up so much in my life, I deserve to live dangerously. At least the computer gives me company. It titillates me and makes me feel alive. I now have companions my own age, these folks in the films. They are all I have right now."

I know Michael well enough to appreciate his all-or-nothing approach, yet it is still difficult to listen to him trashing himself. I do my best to be patient and to gently redirect him toward healthier, more productive stances. He acknowledges that there is another part of him:

"It is lonely and I am at a standstill. Pornography actually is a punishment to me, totally the opposite of what I often tell myself. I should not be doing this. It is taking me away from being with other people. I am spending money I do not have and it is upsetting to admit where I am going when I allow myself to see the big picture. I do not want to sabotage myself anymore. I feel like the circus performer on the trapeze and I need to change."

CRUISING CONFESSIONS

Paul was a client I saw many years ago. After seeing me for months, he finally confessed that there was one last thing he hadn't yet talked about—sex and cruising. It turns out that he would go out on his bike very late at night looking for sex. He came to life during these late evening hours, sometimes lasting to the early hours of the morning. He loved the ritual of going out when the rest of the world was sleeping, seeking out his conquests. He prided himself in being successful in his career, never showing up late for work, and somehow able to deal with his sleep deprivation.

Though he was embarrassed to initiate this conversation with me, he was glad to finally admit it and it enriched his work with me. While discussing this, he had a big smile on his face. It was a smile of pride, as though he were sharing a secret gem with me. Not only did he enjoy the aliveness he felt during these late-night cruises, but he also enjoyed how special it made him feel and sharing that with me .

The Healthy Line

It is important for us to explore the line between healthy sexuality and sexual compulsivity. Sex addicts lose creative/play time. They become detached from art, sports, or other forms of creative and physical expression, and they are often tired, late to work, or take long periods of time out of the workday to pursue sex. As with Paul, some people cruise late into the night, and find that time to be a tantalizing exciting time, while others sit at home online, surfing the internet late at night, discovering new porn sites while downing glasses of wine. (In the latter case, two addictions are fueled simultaneously.)

When a person struggling with sexual compulsivity is caught in a state of intensity, he is in a trance state where all of his internal focus is on a pursuit—the pursuit of sex. It might be found on a computer, in pornography, on a phone app, with an actual person, or through masturbation—the options are potentially captivating. When a compulsive person is in this trance state, everything else recedes. His focus is on that one thing, and he will spend long periods of time in this state of physical and emotional stimulation. .

The Rush

Patrick Carnes accurately describes this trance state: "The addict's mood is altered as he enters the obsessive trance. The metabolic responses are like a rush through the body as androgens speed up the body's functioning." (Carnes, 2001, p. 560)

He goes on to describe how the ritualistic aspects of sex addiction deepen the trance-like experience: "Like a yogi in meditation, the addict does not have to stop and think or disrupt his focus. The ritual itself, like preoccupation, can start the rush of excitement." (Carnes, 2001, p. 573)

The intoxication of the whole experience is what the addict seeks. "In fact, many men are seeking this more than they are orgasm. His relationship to a mood altering experience becomes central to his life." (Carnes, 2001, p. 451)

The person who becomes a sex addict doesn't become one over night. Over time, he finds excitement in the trance experience of acting out. Then, this state continues to furnish him with a distraction from what is going on inside. It feels so powerful and exciting that nothing else really measures up. As a result, he pursues this experience over other activities. Simultaneously, shame and embarrassment about being gay or about sexual activities reinforce the addictive behavior, since these are experienced inside as negative trance states.

Choosing to seek out sex, rather than spending time with friends, dating, or community activities becomes the norm for a sex addict.

IS BEING GAY THE SAME THING AS BEING A SEX ADDICT?

Gay men are not sex addicts because they are gay. As Weiss explains: "It is far more complicated. Genetics, attachments, and emotional coping skills need to be taken into account. It is due to a consequence of individual psychological issues, and neurological predispositions to addiction." (Weiss, 2005, p. 65)

Hedges describes a psychodynamic approach: "All of our compulsions and addictions symbolically mark important experiences of deep satisfaction or frustration in our earliest relationships. Our repetitive sexual fantasies and enactments stand as psychological representations of truly important parts of ourselves that deserve to be cherished, understood, and lived in the most fulfilling ways possible." (Hedges, 2011, p. 146)

Compulsive Masturbation

Because it is a solitary activity, people don't think of masturbation as problematic. However, for those who compulsively masturbate, a great deal of time is spent in seclusion, and day-to-day aspects of life are neglected. The computer becomes the escape. Even the sound of the modem starting becomes sexualized. (Carnes, 2001)

Masturbating for hours on end, sleep deprivation...addicts tell themselves that cybersex is not real and that the people on the computers are not real. (Carnes, 2001) This can be a way of denying addiction.

Weiss sums it up: "Pain, anxiety, anger, fear, and frustration are blunted and discharged through hours of masturbation. Seduction and arousal become replacements for vulnerability and intimacy." (Weiss, 2005, pp. 58- 60)

WHAT DOES YOUR BODY HAVE TO SAY?

Sexually compulsive clients are busy externalizing by focusing on their sexual activities rather than what they are noticing inside themselves. What happens when you think that your client's behaviors may be sexually compulsive, but he doesn't?

The primary goal in helping clients identify their own sexual compulsivity is to elicit self-reflection, as well as honesty, without confronting him. Assessing his behaviors can be difficult due to sexual norms in the gay community and defensiveness as a normal reaction to having his sexual behaviors questioned.

Both conversation and experiential work create the ideal foundation for exploration. Your client will explore the realities of his sexual behavior and acknowledge what is healthy and unhealthy for himself.

This is important: You accomplish this by encouraging your client to decipher the feeling and experience of the state he is in before, during, and after his sexual experiences. You invite him to explore this in detail, and do your best to be free of judgment so that he can have the space to come to his own conclusions. Clients who enjoy experiential work are apt to be less guarded and more honest while doing this in trance.

LISTENING TO YOUR BODY (FOR IDENTIFYING SEXUAL COMPULSIVITY)

Start out with a basic relaxation exercise, and then ask the following questions. Being aware of sensations inside, both emotional and physical, can be key to your clients appreciating how they really feel about their sexual behaviors. Be explicit about breaking the awareness down to before, during, and after.

When your client is relaxed, as these questions:

Before Sex

- What were you thinking about beforehand?
- What did you notice going on inside during this time?
- What physical sensations were you aware of?
- What emotions were you aware of?
- What thoughts did you have about your potential actions?

During Sex

- What were you thinking about during this period of time?
- What did you notice inside your body during this period of time?
- What physical sensations were you aware of?
- What emotions were you were aware of?
- What thoughts did you have about your potential actions?

(Be attentive to the differences in answers from before—to during.)

After Sex

- What were you thinking about afterward?
- What did you notice inside your body?
- What physical sensations were you aware of?
- What emotions were you aware of?
- What thoughts did you have about your actions?

With this type of exploration, clients appreciate there may have been interpersonal, emotional, or traumatic responses that manifest themselves in acting-out behaviors. Based on self-reflection, honest acknowledgement helps with the possibilities of creating and adhering to healthier behaviors. Frequently, powerful insights spontaneously arise.

OTHER SELF-ASSESSMENT TOOLS FOR SEXUAL COMPULSIVITY

For those who prefer a more cognitive approach to self-assessment, there are self-tests available to help identify problematic behaviors. Since this is a sensitive subject, be certain to approach the tests gently, and allow sufficient time to process the significance of doing the tests, both before and after. You and your client can do them together. I usually read the questions aloud and write down the client's responses. You can also have clients answer the questions at home and bring the results to you the following session.

Forty Questions for Self-Diagnosis

Sex and Love Addicts Anonymous (SLAA) is a 12-step program to which I often refer. It provides a list of 40 questions for self-examination (which is available online at 40 Questions for Self Diagnosis-Sex and Love Addicts Anonymous). The questions are an effective tool for self-reflection, and ultimately, self-diagnosis. An added benefit is that the onus isn't solely on the therapist to point out a difficult conclusion, but rather it is the client's own revelations that come to the foreground.

Gay Male Sexual Screening Self-Test

Another good self-test is the Gay Male Sexual Screening Self-Test (G-SAST) for Sex Addiction developed by Patrick Carnes and Robert Weiss. The test presents 25 Yes/No questions that can be scored. It helps gay men identify problems with sex addiction. (Weiss, 2005, p. 32)

It is equally powerful to explore these questions (or the answers to the questions) with clients in session so that they have time to process suspicions or conclusions with you, or to hear your feedback.

Build-Up Script

Derek Polonsky uses a build-up script when asking teens about their sexuality and use of contraception. He begins by asking: "Do you smoke?" or "Do you use seatbelts?" (Polonsky, 2012) Once he gets an idea of how they assess risk for themselves in other areas of their lives, he slowly builds up to his questions regarding sex. By the time he gets to safety and contraception, his clients are less defensive.

I have adapted this approach for gay men, regarding safer sex and also compulsivity. Again, utilization, the hallmark of Ericksonian work, is central. Choose questions that you assume will resonate with the interests of your client. Utilize his preferences to build up to a set of questions.

For example, with many urban gay men who are into their body image and going to the gym, you could ask: "Do you pay attention to what kinds of foods you eat, including carbs and low fat?" For the body conscious person, the answer is most likely yes. You have set up a receptive tone and comfort level for your client in answering yes, and have indirectly implied that taking care of himself is something that he stresses.

For those who don't fit this stereotype, choose attributes that are important to them. Build this into a dialogue so that your client feels positive about answering "yes" questions. This will allow you to create a tone that will automatically minimize defensiveness and encourage receptivity. You will then be able to help your client identify his true motives.

THE STRENGTH OF EGO-STATE WORK WITH SEXUAL COMPULSIVITY

Maybe your sexually compulsive client is willing to acknowledge his struggles regarding sexuality. If he is unwilling to acknowledge them, there are ways that you can intervene that will help him to understand what motivates him sexually; among the most effective is "parts" work.

Sometimes clients who do acknowledge their struggles wish they could just erase the parts of themselves that function less well, for instance, the part that acts out with compulsive sex. Unfortunately, that isn't possible, and wishful thinking isn't helpful.

It is healthier to accept and make room for all. By using the higher functioning parts, one can illuminate how or why the other parts are present, or how to use the more functional parts to help the less functional parts. It is a powerful, practical process to use in therapy.

Furthermore, using parts work with sexual issues motivates clients to compartmentalize less, while also appreciating deeper internal motivations that are healthier. This is more productive than the client giving in to addiction or the therapist having to lecture about it.

Given that sexual addiction is similar to a trance state where one is "unaware of the consequences of his actions and is singularly focused on whatever exciting sexual activity is in front of him" (Weiss, 2005, p. 7), we can intervene by exploring the various ego states that propel our clients. Every sexually compulsive client has parts that don't necessarily want to act out. We can help him to appreciate these parts and use them for maintaining strength and control. We can explore the less strong parts in order for the client to understand what motivates his addiction. As his healthier parts become aligned to lead him back to strength, there is always competition between healthy and less healthy parts. But allowing this to surface, we can guide him to find ways of reconciling by coming up with healthy strategies.

Helping your client delineate these parts is reassuring, less overwhelming, and a great way to assist them in organizing their internal struggles. Ultimately, it is one of the best tools available for understanding and changing behaviors related to sexual compulsivity. Self-judgment lessens as disparate or conflicting parts are no longer diminished. "There are no parts that you should not have," Claire Fredrick repeats in a consultation group that I attend.

As you encourage your clients to do ego-state work, tensions release, dissociative tendencies and compartmentalization diminishes, and a self- organizing presence emerges before your very eyes. It is so quick and powerful that it seems like magic. It isn't, it is ego-state work. It is my preferred mode of working with sexual compulsivity. Learn more about this.

MARC:

Marc struggles with sexual compulsivity and the decision to have unprotected sex. He feels out of balance, frequently using his mobile phone to search for local guys to hook up with. He spends hours each day doing this. He is often distracted by thoughts of what adventures he might find online.

In these encounters, he frequently is a bottom (with anal intercourse) and doesn't use condoms. This risk is distressing to him and he wants to stop putting himself in this kind of danger. "Integration is something that is missing in my life and I cannot figure out why I am blocked. I want to stop having unprotected sex."

We use hypnosis to explore what is blocking his integration. I decide that it would be best to combine trance with ego-state (parts) work.

This is what he first experienced in trance:

"I see luggage where I am storing old memories. There are steamer trunks that are plaid, leather, and striped."

I think of this as his different parts:

"I open one of the pieces of luggage and inside this one is my sexual energy, which I keep top secret."

His challenge is to give himself permission to have his own space, his sexual energy, without acting on it. I was curious what prompted him to equate sexual energy with acting out.

"I am really into bare backing (having unprotected sex with anal intercourse) because it represents a complete freedom from inhibition...something I don't have much of in my life."

"Although I am embarrassed to admit it, it feels kind of cool to imagine being with somebody who is HIV. I fantasize about not worrying whether I will get HIV or not."

"I do admit that I fantasize about this. I link it to having absolute freedom. For me, HIV lingers in a dark place where the grass is greener. This is a dark secret that I don't dare admit to my friends, but I do know that many other people fantasize about the same thing because there are blogs and pornographic websites on this topic."

He is conscious of my presence. "I know how this sounds for you to hear this, but I am just speaking my truth right now. I have a dark side that excites me."

On one hand, it is unsettling to hear him describe this so candidly, yet am also pleased that he is willing to trust me and use his time in therapy to work on this. His honesty and willingness makes it easier for me to persevere in working toward healthier goals with him. I am also intrigued by his compartmentalization and how he has separated parts of himself from other parts; sex is the venue where these separations exist.

The Dark Side Part

He describes: "This is the part of me that is excited yet shameful; hidden, yet uninhibited."

The Naughty Part

"This is the part of me that enjoys doing things that I know shouldn't do. I have been such a people pleaser my whole life, enjoying the role of being responsible, yet I always keep quiet about this naughty part of myself, even with my best gay male friends who know me the most."

The Integrated Part

"This is the opposite of my dark side. It is my ideal self, the person that others actually see in social situations. It takes great energy to maintain this part of myself because others only know me in this role, which is very important for me to maintain." His expression becomes sadder. "My integration part just feels blank these days. My true battle is that I really like my dark side and I truly wish I could keep pursuing it."

By exploring these parts in-depth, and feeling free to express them, there is a kind of relief that seems to overshadow the less healthy parts. Suddenly, he shifts his focus. "I see myself opening a door. I am walking into a room where there is a circle of people that represent a variety of people in my life. In this circle hands are joined and everybody loves me exactly for who I really am, rather than who I pretend to be. They are committed to me."

MAKING SENSE OF IT

This was an important experience for Marc, since much of his history about growing up gay consisted of living in solitary ways. Sexual escapades were pursued, but he considered them to be naughty, which was simultaneously painful and exciting. Perhaps fetishizing about being part of the HIV population recapitulated his feeling of being naughty and exciting. It was also a way of not being alone.

In doing hypnosis, he enjoyed being part of his own group, front and center. This group was where he could experience himself in a healthy way. He could now be free, instead of naughty.

The ego-state work enabled him to make changes and to set healthier goals for himself.

His goals:

- Delete the online accounts from his phone that serve as distractions.
- Contact me if he feels he is in danger of slipping.

- Only use porn sites that have visual images without interactive elements.
- Allow others to get to know him better, including close friends, in order to demystify his dark and naughty parts.
- Join a gay therapy group where members can support him in these struggles.
- Get HIV tested in a timely manner.

Providing this client with the setting in which to be intimate and honest, while also encouraging ego-state work, allowed him to let go of his secrets and decide how to make progress. It has been two years since he delineated and fulfilled these promises.

USING AN EGO-STATE SCRIPT FOR SEXUAL COMPULSIVITY

In traditional Ericksonian fashion, the best way to do parts work is to do it your own way. My script suggestions can be used as a guide, but translating them into your own language will provide the personal touch necessary to resonate with your clients.

This piece will help the client organize and keep track of his awareness. Each part contains its own distinct sensory sensations that differ from those of the other parts. Being able to make these distinctions will feel like an almost magical shift for the client. Being able to make space for all parts will be a relief. As a therapist, you will more easily intervene with curiosity, instead of judgment.

I will describe the case of Marc to clarify the use of this script, and then present the script itself.

Me:

- "You say that you enjoy bare backing and that it excites you. What would you call this part of yourself?"
- Alternatively, and using his language: "You refer to your dark side...is there something else you might call this part?"
- "You also say that you are spending hours checking phone apps looking to meet guys. What would you call this part?" (He an-

swered, "the naughty part.")

- "And, you also said that integration is missing and that you wanted to stop having unsafe anal intercourse. What would you call this part? (He answered it was his integrated part.)
- "Are there other parts of which you are aware?"

I then focused on each part and asked him explore his sensory awareness with each of these parts. I asked him to appreciate experiencing these parts by seeing and understanding them as parts of a greater whole—as if there was a family living inside him.

IDENTIFYING THE PARTS

Starting with a basic induction and deepening, you can help the client to identify his parts by repeating his words:

"You were saying that you [________].What would you call this part of you?" (Encourage the client to use his creativity and to put it into his own words, in a way that is clear and concise.) Or, "Can you identify what this part is in just a word or two?"

- "You also said [_______]. What would you call this part?" Or, "What would you call the part of you that [________]?" (Continue this until you have covered all of what your client considers, or until he doesn't imagine any other parts.)
- "There might be more...does anything else come to you?" (I write each of these parts down so I can remember them; this also shows that I take the parts seriously.)
- "Just focus on each of these parts separately. Notice what comes to you, what you feel (with regard to this part), what thoughts are in your awareness, or what is happening physically inside your body in this moment, or any images that you are aware of." (The more you emphasize these sensory modalities, the more detailed the answers will be.)
- "Describe your awareness of having all these parts existing to-

gether, with each other." Or, "What do you see?" "What do you feel?" (I refer to this as "big picture awareness," where clients can step back and see the totality of parts in a different context, rather than just individual parts.

HYPNOSIS: A HEALTHIER TRANCE STATE

Since the search for the high—an unhealthy state—is a component with sexual compulsivity, you can encourage the use of experiential work as an alternate trance state—a healthy state. Help your client recognize that he chooses to exist in a healthier state rather than finding unhealthy avenues of escape.

BRUCE:

As Bruce is assessing whether or not he is sexually compulsive, I incorporate the "Listening to Your Body Script," presented earlier. Once I knew he was receptive to this exploration, I quickly continued.

In trance, I ask him to describe moments in his life when he was aware of finding distractions that were good for him. I ask him to describe the ways that he knew it was healthy for him, as well as the ways in which he felt good at the time. I ask him to focus on his sensory awareness:

"I love running. It is a healthy endeavor that I really enjoy."

I ask him to imagine enjoying the sounds of his sneakers hitting the ground as he is running, or the sounds of the treadmill at the gym where he sometimes runs. He smiles.

I invite him to notice the way in which his sneakers absorb the impact of his body as they hit the ground. (This is a nice metaphor for being able to absorb the impact of life in healthy way, versus acting out.)

I also ask him to focus on the feeling in his chest as he is running—how his healthy breathing is deeply in synch and rhythmic, and that his body knows just what to do, without even thinking about it.

As his comfort develops, I increase the significance of the exercise. I ask to hear about situations that weren't the healthiest for him. Once he is receptive, I get him to focus on the internal feelings that he is aware of. I want him to pay particular attention to the shift that he experiences between each of these states—healthy and not so healthy. His strong alliance with me during this experience, along with his honest inventory of himself, provide a powerful awareness of how acting out sexually by having anonymous sex is something he doesn't want to do anymore.

He follows this with, "I now understand things so much more clearly. My sexual behavior has not been healthy, even though I have been pretending it is just fine."

Script: Healthy Distractions

Start with a basic trance. Once the client is relaxed, you can continue with the Healthy Distractions Script.

Remember a moment in your past, when you were able to shift your focus away from stress or discomfort, in a healthy way that you knew was good for you. Excellent. [If you prefer, you can mention a moment that you know worked well for your client.]

This may have been an activity, or even a place you go to. It feels good to shift this focus for yourself, right here, right now, that is right.

Experience what has come to you, such as thoughts, images, or sensations. Appreciate the ways that you now feel as you remember this moment. Your body and mind feel healthy, you feel good. [You can ask the client what he has come up with.]

Shifting focus:

Now allow yourself to notice distractions or behaviors that you know really aren't the best ones for you. As we both know, everybody has these. [You can give examples of other people who make choices that are problematic for them. You can ask the client what he comes up with.]

Notice what you feel inside now, such as the thoughts, images, or sensations you are aware of. That's right.

You can acknowledge whatever painful feelings emerge, and you can really appreciate your own ability to be honest with yourself. Excellent. I wonder if your ability to be honest with yourself feels like a relief.

SHIFTING FOCUS BACK TO THE FIRST STATE:

I wonder if you can bring yourself back to the first place you chose, the place where you can bring yourself away from stress, in pleasurable or healthy ways. Excellent.

Once again, just experience what has come to you, such as thoughts, images, or sensations. Appreciate the ways that you feel now.

I wonder if there is a way in which your body feels more relaxed... notice the relief. That's right.

Appreciate the ways in which it feels different to engage in these different kinds of escapes—some healthy, others not.

And you know, you can use our own strength, your own abilities to find healthy distractions for yourself whenever you want, whenever you need.

HELPING YOUR CLIENT PLAN FOR HEALTHIER SEX

If you sense that your client needs more structure in attaining sexual sobriety, you can use "A Sexual Boundary Plan," devised by Weiss. (Weiss, 2005) In this, he identifies three distinct boundaries: Inner, Middle, and Outer.

- *The Inner Boundary* – This is your client's bottom line, consisting of the most damaging behaviors, including sexual acts, use of pornography, or masturbation that is destructive.
- *The Middle Boundary*—These are actions or situations that will likely lead to acting out sexually. If your client is able to be honest with himself long before meeting his bottom line, he can then anticipate and plan on how to maintain control.
- *The Outer Boundary*—This includes the rewards people receive from healthy choices, such as recovery, or life-enhancing activi-

ties like social connections, family, gym time, and creative pursuits.

The goal in planning for healthier sex is to simultaneously strengthen these three boundaries. Clients often need to be reminded that healthier choices include finding activities (outside of acting out) that are healthy and rewarding. Often addicts aren't attuned to this.

I also stress regular group meetings such as Sex and Love Addicts Anonymous (SLAA), sexual addiction group therapy, or a general therapy groups for gay men, where compulsivity is addressed routinely and support is provided.

MOTIVATIONAL INTERVIEWING

Whether your clients are working on sexual compulsivity, attachment issues, or gay sexual norms that might be unhealthy for them, using motivational interviewing is effective. Skill building is the aim.

I enjoy the marriage of motivational interviewing and Ericksonian psychotherapy, both approaches based on the use of tailoring. Standardized prevention messages can be perceived as confrontational; these strategies prove to be more effective in that they account specifically for individual circumstances and personalities.

This goes to Jeff Zeig's point: "Focus the therapy through the patient's lens, speak the patient's experiential language, and ascertain how the patient does strengths and lives strengths and use that as part of the therapeutic intervention." (Gil, 2004)

Mr. Fix-It

Sometimes I struggle with this partnership when my clients engage in risky sex or compulsive sexuality. My stance becomes more authoritative than casual, and I take it upon myself to "fix" things. Sometimes confrontation shuts things down; avoiding it may open the space for building motivation and confidence in moving forward.

Motivational interviewing assumes that clients feel ambivalent about unhealthy behaviors. They may not openly verbalize this, but if we can get to that, either through the use of hypnosis or gentle questions used in motivational interviewing, then there will be an important shift in their treatment.

Frequently, I use ego-state work in conjunction with motivational interviewing. Breaking down the part of him that is willing to take risks and enjoys it, while exploring another part of him – one that might be ambivalent or feel badly about the behavior eases my dictatorial and judgmental tone. More is accomplished as a result.

Some key principles used in motivational interviewing include:

- *Expression of empathy.*
- *Helping clients shape their behaviors.* Using encouragement any time a client makes even just a little change.
- *Assessing and Reflecting.* "How important is it for you to personally change this, and can you rate this on a scale from 0–10?" You ask the client to rate the importance of each sexual behavior, and then have him rate his own confidence regarding these behaviors.
- *Using a decision matrix.* "Can you tell me what you like about your current behavior, and can you tell me what you don't like about your current behavior?"

Then, "Did I miss anything? Is there anything more that you would like to add?"

These are powerful final questions, since you are inviting him to share more, rather than telling him to remember what he forgot.

Sitting With the Information

It can be difficult for clinicians to hear about the details of clients' adventures, and equally difficult knowing how to best intervene.

Remember, it is not your job to police your client's behavior. As much as you want to make sure that your client understands that his issue is sexual compulsivity, the push to make him understand or acknowledge it just keeps you stuck in an uncomfortable struggle. Instead, do your best to be there to assist him in appreciating why he chooses to act on his sexual feelings. You might wonder, What is going on that he may be avoiding? Why is he spending so much time pursuing this? How does he really feel deep inside about his behavior?

Shame isn't always what clients experience. Clients may feel proud to share the details of their conquests in therapy, or perhaps they are unaware of the impact that this sharing has on us. Finding a position of tolerance without reinforcing that his behaviors are okay is tricky. Corbett comments on this: "Was I to be proud of his willful ignorance of the other's desires and personhood? Or was I to feel pride at his capacity to find men who wished to surrender to his desire?" (Corbett, 2009, p. 225)

SEXUAL COMPULSIVITY: THE CHALLENGE TO THERAPY

Maintaining care and respect for your client can be a difficult. At the same time, care and respect are key ingredients in all treatment success. Nowhere is this more important than in the sphere of sexual compulsivity. The client's dedication, even his seeming pride in unhealthy, sometimes dangerous exploits can frustrate and anger anyone trying to be of help.

Combining the various modes outlined in this chapter, along with the experiential work, can ease the therapeutic relationship and create enough positive regard for change to happen.

Not every client will embrace your approach. Remember to ask for help when you need it. Get consultation, or send your clients for outside consults. Utilize the assistance of screening tests groups such as SLAA or group therapy, as well as education, so that your client can begin to assess his situation honestly. Insights that come from the inside are preferable to ones that come from you. Your client will have a better chance of initiating the changes that can then be maintained because the roots are internal.

CHAPTER EIGHT
The Shadow of HIV

Perhaps you are wondering if HIV still needs to be the topic of its own chapter. The worst of HIV, meaning the severity of illness and the greatest number of deaths, occurred in the 1980s and '90s. With breakthroughs in medications and treatment protocols people are now living healthier and longer. For many, the pain of the epidemic has been buried somewhere in history and the cruel memories forgotten.

I have chosen to go into detail about HIV for a few reasons. First of all, the ways in which HIV affected the gay male community are profound and enduring; we wouldn't be where we are, or who we are, if HIV didn't exist. The epidemic radically influenced the essence of the gay male community. Using experiential work for gay men to realize this is expedient and freeing. The examples in this chapter portray this. Any medical or mental health provider working with gay men needs to be aware of the impact of HIV, in order to provide services that are informed, viable, and current.

The second reason is based on my ongoing premise that gay men have spent too much time concealing themselves. If we ignore HIV, we encourage the old ways of coping: compartmentalization and silence. True healing comes from unwrapping the layers of protection in order to live more whole lives. HIV awareness is part of that unwrapping.

Even though the landscape of HIV has drastically shifted over the years, its experiential impact needs to be remembered by gay men of all ages. As you read this, you will come to better appreciate how HIV has affected gay men, and it will help you in your clinical practice.

Finally, people are still getting diagnosed with HIV and need services and support. You can assist them by knowing what is important to emphasize and how to support them.

LAWRENCE:

Lawrence returned to therapy because he felt that his daily life was lacking in mindfulness. He was getting caught up in trying to advise people how they should run their lives, not paying as much attention to his own. Even though he had done grief work years ago, due to losing friends to HIV, he realized that he had yet another layer of grief with which to deal.

In the following excerpts, take note of the ways in which Lawrence came up with new meanings, and how spontaneous it was with the help of trance.

"I have been through so much caring for my sick friends. With these challenges, I learned that I couldn't keep a person from dying. Instead, I honored their wishes, with patience and acceptance. It wasn't an easy lesson."

"I have had so many hospital scenarios where I was always trying to change and fix things—getting Brett a new ID card; Jay asking me to take his IV bags and throw them away, which I did; and holding Dan at his dying weight of only 90 pounds. Turning him over, he whispered into my ear and said he did not want to do it anymore and I said, okay. I prayed Al would pass away so I would not have to make the decision to take him off the ventilator."

Lawrence states that there is still a lingering last part of grief. "I can have a role in my own destiny!" Somehow, in his previous grief work he hadn't fully allowed himself to own this part. Perhaps life back then felt too precarious, but it is different now—life is his now.

Hypnosis continues...and so do the metaphors that provide so much clarity.

"I am alone because people have left. I see pathways leading to a circle, which is protected by a membrane. The membrane is stretched in the shape of a circle and represents the protection I have from being on the other side of it. My friends that died are on the inside and I am on the outside. It is comforting to know that I can come and go, moving away from this circle when my busy life calls me, yet stay near the circle and be safe under my tree on this side. I am not keeping things at bay anymore because my guardian angels can easily travel in and out. They are letting me have the wisdom of knowing that I am a tough cookie and I persevere. I watch over them in a comforting way. There is a joy for me in acknowledging the vastness of the universe. Life is much bigger and I am much bigger than I have realized."

As he comes out of trance he adds, "This lesson is inside of me now." These few words explain why hypnosis is helpful.

Lawrence now appreciates the importance of mindfulness more than ever and is able to practice it more fully.

HIV IN THE PAST

Any gay male who was out in the early '80s or prior remembers the horror of that era. The mysterious illness, initially called GRID (Gay Related Infectious Disease), and later referred to AIDS or ARC, depending upon the severity of the illness, was a killer. Randy Shilts from his book, *And The Band Played On*: "People died and nobody paid attention because the mass media did not like covering stories about homosexuals and was especially skittish about stories that involved gay sexuality." (Balter, 1996; Shilts, 2007)

Most men who were diagnosed were dead within two years. It was traumatic for the community. There was a lot of hysteria, not just among gay men, but also in the community at large. People didn't know how contagious AIDS was and how it was transmitted. Gay men became even more isolated, as their families stayed away.

Many young men were losing friends and battling their own

health simultaneously. Some were afraid to get tested, and others, though perfectly healthy, were plagued by AIDS anxiety, even if they believed they weren't infected. Anxiety needs a hook on which to rest, and fears regarding AIDS became the ideal hook—a place where religion, shame, homophobia, and ignorance about gay male sexuality could intricately intertwine.

I myself came out in the early '80s and remember the fears I experienced as I read articles in *Newsweek* and *Time*. The promises and freedom of being newly out were tainted with fears about death. However, being out and working in Boston gave me the opportunity to give back to my community by running volunteer support groups and eventually running a group program to meet the mental health needs of people affected by HIV.

As I was emerging in the field of mental health, I could offer gay males something that older gay males couldn't: youth. I could sit with a man who was infected, dying, or anxious, and not simultaneously be dealing with it in my friendship network, whereas my older peers weren't as lucky. Many of them either were infected themselves, or were losing friends and lovers.

I had a 360-degree view of AIDS, since I was working with clients who had HIV, supporting healthcare providers around the pain of treating these patients, educating mental health providers on the psychosocial issues of HIV, and supporting family members to prepare for their loved one's death. I will always remember the intensity and the pain of working with so many relatively young dying men, bereaving families and friends, and the stigmas that surrounded gay male sexuality.

People were ill and dying throughout the urban gay community. Healthcare facilities and hospitals were in a state of crisis. Some families learned about a relative being gay when the phone rang and the person on the other end told of his illness or passing. In that era, many men who had HIV preferred to call it cancer, since even cancer was considered more acceptable.

However, the truth is, HIV did bring the community together in wonderful ways. Gay men, characteristically portrayed as being shallow, were coming together, and other groups of compassionate people were joining them to fight the epidemic. The gay male community coalesced like never before.

Show Me the Money: The Viatical Settlement

A creative accommodation to gay male pressures to live well even when the person was ill or dying, came in the form of the viatical settlement. Gay men would sell their existing life insurance policies to a third party. It was considered a win-win situation. Many gay men had substantial life insurance policies, either because they had the foresight to invest in one, or the company where they worked offered good benefits. Since many gay men in that era did not have children, selling their policies proved to be profitable, given their diminished life expectancy. The seller would receive a lump sum, which was a percentage of what the policy was worth, with life expectancy taken into account. Third-party investors would assume the monthly premiums and would cash out when the person died, hence receive the other portion. At the time, because men were dying so quickly, investors did well in a relatively short period of time.

Gay men who "cashed out" often did well too. Some bought homes, or second homes, or third homes. Others were able to get by more comfortably and could pay for their own funeral and burial expenses.

WHAT IF WE FIND A CURE?

In 1996, *Science* magazine announced the "Breakthrough of the Year," introducing a new cocktail used to treat HIV, called "protease inhibitors." (Balter, 1996) In many instances, "combined therapy (with protease inhibitors) has led to the inability to any longer detect the virus within treated patients. And, while it is certainly recognized that such treatment does not offer a cure for the disease, the treatment does for the first time offer significant hope that HIV infections might at least be managed sufficiently to allow a reasonable life for many who suffer from this disease."

I remember this time vividly. I was in a monthly peer support group for mental health clinicians who lead HIV groups. We heard about the soon-to-be released protease inhibitors and were all wondering what this would mean to both clinicians and patients. It sounded like a dream come true—a combination "cocktail" that would prolong people's lives.

The details of HIV were about to change dramatically. Patients and therapists had more than 10 years to get the nuances of living and dying with HIV down, and we did. Suddenly, dying of HIV might be taken off the table. Could this promise be trusted? Our hopes for cures had been shattered before.

Indeed, this marked the beginning of a new landscape. It could never be a return to the old one, before people started dying, but it looked brighter. AIDS patients taking protease inhibitors had higher T-cell counts and viral loads that were undetectable, or nearly undetectable. Over the years, the cocktails have continued to improve. People now are living much longer and it has changed the landscape of HIV.

Many patients who were once expecting to die went back to work and felt a sense of normalcy again. Those who didn't come out to their family about having HIV didn't necessarily need to, and there was and continues to be, a growing list of long-term survivors. This is a phrase that is happily used, especially since many didn't expect the added longevity. It hasn't come without costs though. Common side effects from long-term use of protease inhibitors include gastrointestinal disturbances, skin problems, insulin resistant diabetes, hepatitis viruses, and lipodystrophy, as well as an increased risk of heart disease...to name a few. (Gil, 2004)

THE HEALTHY LOOK OF MASCULINITY

One part of HIV treatment was testosterone. Low testosterone is prevalent among men with HIV, and whether by injection, patches, or gels, it has been commonly prescribed to increase muscle mass, and increase energy and sexual functioning.

Now, what do you think of when you think of testosterone? One image that comes to mind is certainly a muscular hyper-masculine look. So, many men were suddenly looking ripped, with thick, beautiful muscles. Logically, the "treatment" then caught on in the mainstream. "Steroid use by men who are HIV positive, who often then build and sculpt their bodies as a fringe benefit of the steroids, has perhaps normalized black market steroid use by HIV negative men." (Signorile, 1998, p. 139-40; Creswell, 2009)

Doctors treating gay men in the '90s reported an increase in steroid use and abuse. The social scene—circuit parties where A-list gay men gathered in popular destinations such as New York City, Miami, or San Francisco, to dance, do drugs, stay up all night and meet similar gay men—was going strong. It wasn't enough to go to the gym to keep up, steroids provided the extra help.

In the early '90s, a huge circuit event happened during the July 4th week in Provincetown, Massachusetts (where I live). There were parties throughout the week and men bursting with muscles arrived from all over the world. The look was one for which gay men strived—and, of course, in most cases failed to achieve. One client, strikingly handsome (recall the discussion of gay men having distorted ideas about their appearance), bemoaned: "I am trying to hang on to any shred of self-esteem that I have." (Thank heavens it wasn't just me!)

Testosterone had been used to treat the side effects of HIV, but it also changed the mainstream appearance of gay men. It placed additional pressure on men already vulnerable with self-esteem issues, even further endangering their well-being.

FACES OF HIV

Every illness possesses three important components. The first component relates to coping with the illness itself which includes medical treatments, protocols, diminishing health, fears about the future, etc. The second component is mourning the loss of the identification of the healthy self—the once healthy person becomes vulnerable, sick, and less able. The third component is sharing the process of the illness with loved ones, who experience their own worry and sense of loss.

What has made HIV unique, particularly when one thinks of contemporary life in Western society, is that people may be dealing with their own illness, while simultaneously coping with the illness or death of friends or partners.

Another lesson, which is hardly exclusive to HIV, is the moving target of what is the client's standard of an acceptable quality of life. Prior to decline, clients often discuss with great certainty what they will allow and tolerate, and when they choose to die. However, when they reach these milestones, they usually continue their quest to live; what once seemed intolerable becomes bearable. As therapists, we need not to be surprised when this happens.

MALCOLM:

A long-term AIDS survivor, Malcolm, comes to me for depression related to his illness. He arrives at my office hobbling on two canes. He is gasping for breath, moving very slowly and in a great deal of physical pain. It appears as though he is ready for death. My work in the '80s has prepared me for this situation.

We decide that hypnosis may help with pain management and also help him reconcile some of the loose ends in his life.

The moment he engages in trance, he is vibrantly alive again. I, too, am in my own trance state while working with him. I actually imagine him leaving my office without the canes after the first session.

Week One: "I feel the breath going into my lungs into a place that it could not go before. I feel a deeper commitment to enjoying the very end of each inhale and the end of each exhale. It is delicious, like a ripe summer peach."

I am delighted. He shifts from pain to pleasure in seconds. As is often the case, once he is able to get beyond pain, the bigger picture of existence shows itself more clearly.

"Every day is a day of mourning. When I leave my house I realize how much I am deteriorating and how many things I will not be able to do again, like a walk on the beach or taking the dog for a run. My whole life is now spent going to and from hospitals. There is a lot of work to do before I die. I am not sure why I have to live like this."

My challenge is to allow him to grieve and to experience the painful aspects of his current life, while guiding him to a happier resourceful part that can accept dying.

Week Two: "I feel something good, like satisfaction on the inside or a light covering my chest. This [his chest] is where the pain came from, and now it is the same place that the happiness comes from. I am filled with hope. As a result, part of my depression can disappear now. I see a couch that is overstuffed and big like a cloud, with room all round it, for me and my dog. The windows are open. I feel breeze and enjoy the quiet. I can hear waves, and the couch holds me, like being in a cloud, and my body melds into it. It is perfect comfort."

Week Three: When I see Malcolm the following week, he comments that he vacillates between feeling happy and not having the right to feel happy, based on his history of trauma and being gay. This is the upside of seeing and feeling nuances beyond just pain.

"There is an old messenger who says, 'You do not have a right to be happy.'" Our new mission is to instill the right of happiness inside of him.

In trance, he reports, "I feel this amazing sense of physical openness! It is a joy that is different from happiness. It is clean and light. My heart and my body will eventually break down, but I know I have work to do beforehand, and I will do it. The end of my life will come like Santa and bring me joy. Decompression with dignity! When I die is out of my hands, and several of my friends and family [who have already died] will come to greet me. I find that comforting." He is smiling; his voice is smooth and his body appears relaxed.

Week Four: The fourth session starts off bleak. I visit him at his home since he isn't feeling well.

"How did my life come to this? I see a path to the beach, and I see myself heading into the dunes. This is a place of great memories and happy times. The warmth of the sun and sand on my skin always feels amazing. I am on top of a spectacular sunny, warm hill. But, being in this beautiful place reminds me of my limitations. I cannot get past my physical challenges. I won't be able to go to this place anymore."

At that moment his dog barks, just one quick high-pitched yelp, and he is immediately responsive to it. "My dog takes me away from this space." The dog's intervention is perfect.

"I guess instead of the beach, I can be on my porch and enjoy the sun while I lie on my chair and see the sky. Now is the time to move on. I will grasp reality and do all that I can to please myself."

Week Five: Malcolm is well enough to come to my office. It is a joyous day for him. He was able to drive, to enjoy the summer sky, and he makes it down the steps to my office. As we are talking, the sky becomes darker. Suddenly, we are in the midst of the strongest storm I have ever experienced in 14 years of living on Cape Cod.

We decide to enjoy the storm by going into trance and appreciating the noises and experiences of thunder. His words: "This downpour is cleansing!" He begins to sing: "Oh happy days, oh happy days, wash all the sins away!" He is positively giddy as he bellows: "Give it to the storm, let the storm carry it away. It takes anger and frustration away. The bird takes away depression and flies away. Let the storm carry it away!"

Week Six: The start of this session is unremarkable, but while in trance he describes the following:

"I am experiencing myself going into a tunnel. I am seeing the light, my chest feels so great and heaviness is lifted." He is moaning with pleasure, repeating the description and continuing to moan. I am a bit taken aback and gently suggest a way to have him come out of trance without rushing the session. I do not want him to die! But he responds, "I do not want to come back. I do not want to come back." Once he does, however, he explains that he wanted to let go in hypnosis, and indeed, it felt as though he were dying and a part of him wanted to allow this.

We close this powerful session. The plan we agree on is that he will write down what he wants for his funeral, what should be done with his remains, and what he needs to clean up, regarding some complicated relationships that have kept him stuck in his ill feelings.

Soon, he forgot about his sessions. He had received what he needed from therapy, and had connected with his own strength, so he left therapy. We were both delighted.

MENTAL HEALTH TREATMENT: WHAT WORKED THEN, WHAT WORKS NOW

Since the landscape of HIV has changed over the years, so have the needs in treatment. Years ago, it was preparing for illness and death, and now the model focuses more on managing the physical and emotional symptoms, and using prevention techniques to maintain good health. Medical adherence and depression are key issues.

The Best Approach: A Mind/Body Approach

In the late '80s, Ann Webster, of Benson-Henri Institute for Mind Body Medicine, designed a 10-week mind-body program for HIV. It was revolutionary at the time, one of the first in the nation. The curriculum, along with her enthusiasm and devotion to her clients, created a successful model that is still used today with great success. In fact, research now shows something that she probably had been aware of all along: a mindfulness meditation program, along with attending a stress reduction group, can reduce the decline of T- cells in HIV patients. (Creswell, 2009) Another behavioral medicine study reveals that during an eight-week behavioral medicine group that emphasized biofeedback, guided imagery, and hypnosis, HIV-related symptoms, such as fever, fatigue, pain, headache, nausea and insomnia, decreased and patients' health became more robust. (Auerbach, 1992)

Mind-body approaches remind people of their strengths and allow them to be in charge, rather than just reacting or living in the doom of diagnosis. Ann Webster's group model encompasses the mind-body connection, including teaching clients about stress and its warning signs, relaxation and meditation, and psychoneuroimmunology studies that promote immune functioning. Clients are also given homework assignments. Resiliency, cognitive reframing, emphasis on social support, and relapse prevention should also included. Webster's work is a reminder that helping to motivate a client requires a more practical and positive approach than simply commiserating with them about how horrible it is that they are ill.

Since hypnosis and relaxation are shown to have a prophylactic value for cellular immunity when used before a stressor, these techniques should be employed when clients are facing doctors' visits, family visits, or other stressful situations. Psychotherapy that enhances personal relationships, decreases distress, or enhances self-efficacy, which has positive effects on immunity. (Kiecolt-Glaser, 1992)

Many studies prove the potency of mind-body work. It couldn't be any clearer that support is crucial, and combining experiential work with teaching clients how to maintain healthy habits is the wellspring of successful treatment.

Script: Enhancing Comfort

This is a basic script that can be adapted to suit the context and the client's style. Remember to use comfort, confidence, and the strength of your own voice to emphasize optimism.

You can appreciate the way in which your body is sitting comfortably in this moment. Take your time to breathe deeply and relax. Enjoy the ways in which it feels comfortable to sit here right now, to appreciate how it feels as you take the space and create the time, to be quiet, and mindful. That is right.

You can enjoy the sensations of relaxation. There may be moments where you forget to be attentive to this part of yourself, to your mind, your body and your emotional self. You can benefit from moments like this. Stillness, quietness, and relaxation really provide a great benefit to you. That is right.

And you know, there are many ups and downs throughout various days of your life, like the bouncing of a ball, up and down, up and down. Even though you would wish you felt perfect, day in and day out, life isn't like that. You can endure these ups and these downs with strength, and you know how strong you can be. In fact, you might even remember a time in your past when you felt uncertain about your own sense of strength, and yet, you were able to get beyond a struggle, due to your own natural strengths.

As you remember this time, allow yourself in this moment to enjoy the physical sensations you feel inside. Remember, you can have passing moments of comfort inside, and they can last for longer periods of time each time you practice this, because of your own existing strength.

Inside of you, in the back of your mind, are all kinds of memories and experiences that might even remind you that you have had the ability to cope and to be strong, to be strong and to grow many times already in your life.

This might even include being gay, taking the risk to acknowledge to yourself that you are gay, doing what was best for you, coming out to others. Doing whatever you knew worked just right for you.

And you can continue to do this for yourself now as well. I wonder if you can envision your future by seeing your healthy self in the future, right at this moment. You don't have to strive for perfection; you know that comfort will do just fine for you. You can see yourself in the future, feeling comfortable, feeling strong, being confident in your own abilities to get through each day, each week, each month, with certainty, strength, and good health. That is right.

Just as you knew long ago about the ups and downs of life, and how you could use your strength back then, you can use your strength right now to keep yourself moving forward, to enjoy the momentum of time as it unfolds, to appreciate the growing sense of strength inside you that continues, and continues, and continues along. Excellent!

(To incorporate if your client is feverish.)

You can remember dipping into a nice clear lake of cool water, on a summer day, when you felt so hot that you wanted to cool yourself down. How refreshing that clear water was to your body as you went into the water. How enjoyable it felt to be able to bring yourself to coolness. How immediately and in this moment too, everything can feel better.

(To incorporate if your client is chilled.)

Or, you can also appreciate the feeling of sitting by a fire in the wintertime. How the wood crackling sounded, or how the orange embers glowed, throwing off heat from the flames of the fire which provided warmth, not only to your body, but to your emotional self too.

HIV NOW

Due to the effectiveness of protease inhibitors, many think of HIV as a chronic illness that can be managed, with life expectancy being much greater than it used to be. Younger gay men, in their 30s or younger, haven't lived through the devastating days of HIV. As a result, they don't know of its seriousness the same way that older gay men do. I often compare it to the Polio epidemic in my lifetime. Polio was something older people had, not me. It was an illness I didn't fully understand.

Younger men are willing to engage in riskier sexual behaviors because they can rationalize that there are treatment choices for HIV that weren't available before. In the previous chapter I spoke about the interplay between unsafe sex and attachment difficulties. Gay men are sometimes willing to take the risk of having unsafe sex in order to win another man's love.

Then, there is the older generation of gay men who survived the early days of AIDS. For many, there is a survivor mentality that enables them to engage in risky behaviors. "I lived through it then, what do I have to lose now?" Or, "If I didn't get infected then, why would I get infected now, or need to worry about it now?"

However, the risks of HIV continue to be high, and gay men, both younger and older, are getting infected with HIV (along with other sexually transmitted diseases), at alarmingly high rates.

There may even be some survivor guilt at play for older men. With so many friends and lovers and colleagues gone, we might wonder if surviving has a hidden price.

Many HIV-positive men never expected to become old. In a way, they are unprepared for wrinkles and weight gain and losing hair, all the things that come with longevity. Sometimes we need to metaphorically hold up a mirror to our clients—perhaps creating a script around this reflection—and share some of the deeper things that we see when we look at them.

Samuel, now in his 60s, an age he never thought he'd be, has a trunk full of "sick clothes." These were the pants and shirts he bought so that he'd have them when he lost weight, due to his illness. Now healthy and even a little chubby, he still has the clothes in his closet "just in case." The illness may recede, but the fear doesn't.

DISCORDANT COUPLES

This is a complicated topic, which could easily fill a book. I will stay within the general topic to provide a hint of what needs to be considered.

Myriad issues include the sexual challenges of adopting safer sex practices and self-disclosure for each partner since individual needs for support may differ. Painful conversations will take place, including what needs to happen if the HIV-infected partner becomes ill (medical wishes), and how each member wants his family to be involved during times of illness or death.

When you meet with couples where one partner has HIV, or work with one partner individually, you want to provide an honest and safe forum that encourages the exploration of all these details. Under these circumstances, couples therapy is useful.

"Healthy denial" is a term I like sharing with my clients. Living responsibly to address the significance of getting good medical care, engaging in healthy sex (including safer sexual practices), and taking care of oneself to live a balanced life are all important. And living life as a whole person, rather than just an HIV-patient, is a healthy way to live. Often, we are taught that compartmentalization is not a good way to live, but there is healthy compartmentalization, which many of us actually encourage when we do experiential work. Being prepared for what may come along down the road is a good thing, but living life as a healthy, strong male plays an important role in prevention.

NEWLY DIAGNOSED

Being newly diagnosed may not be the death sentence it was several years ago, but it is still an emotionally painful experience. A lot of important decisions need to be made, including where to find the best medical care. Finding a clinic or hospital that has current treatment protocols is essential. In addition, for men who haven't come out to their physicians, or revealed their HIV status, it is essential to do so. Or, they can switch providers to be able to address the significant issues unique to those with HIV. I have worked with some men who have kept their long-term family physician without disclosing that they are gay, and others who have ignored their HIV status for years because it brings up too much shame or fear.

Undoubtedly, there is great deal of stigma and judgment toward men who in this day and age seroconvert. "Shouldn't they know better"? This is the common question that medical personnel and therapists ask each other. I can't help but wonder how transparent these thoughts may be on our faces, as we sit with clients who are already experiencing so much pain. Of course, factors such as the use of substances and attachment needs, influence decisions regarding unsafe sex made in the heat of the moment.

We know how AIDS is transmitted, and gay men have a choice: adhering to safer sex guidelines to prevent getting HIV, or taking the risk. It seems dangerous to take the risk, yet there are many complicated reasons why men do. You need to ask yourself when working with those who seroconvert: Are you going to come in as another person who judges, or do you have something else to offer?

BOB:

Bob is newly diagnosed. He states in his first session, "I want to kick the debris away from my past to clear the way to my future." But in Bob's second session he identifies drinking and sex as issues he wants to work on. "You fall into things rather than choose things."

Bob has discovered that he is HIV positive, a diagnosis that surprised him. Though doing quite well emotionally, he finds that he is feeling anxious, sleeping poorly, uncertain about sharing his diagnosis, with, and feeling overwhelmed. We decide to use hypnosis as a method for relaxation and mindfulness. I use a basic script, since the goal is simple relaxation.

He realizes: "I am not appreciating things as much as I should. I can resolve it by being more appreciative and living in the moment more."

The following week he continues to report doing well, though in hypnosis he states: "This is your fault Bob. You are a bad boy." I have heard my clients express this type of self-blame many times before.

As much as I would have liked to be Detective Rick and explore with him how he got HIV, with whom and when, at that moment, the most important thing was to help him experience comfort.

"Here are the lessons I have learned about having HIV," he says. "To appreciate more of the good things that I actually have in my life, and to enjoy the positive impact of things. I previously felt lost and threatened, but I don't anymore."

In the next few weeks he gets retested and his numbers are great. The combination of medications, a good attitude, and making meaning out of his diagnosis was helpful to him.

WHAT TO ADDRESS WITH NEWLY DIAGNOSED CLIENTS:

1) To whom should they disclose their HIV status?

Since people aren't necessarily becoming ill following diagnosis, it is reasonable for your clients to decide not to tell their family members or even friends, if they don't feel ready or deem it necessary. I suggest that they have a couple of sources (such as friends or peers) to confide in, since uncertainty is considered typical.

Having plenty of time to prioritize readiness for self-disclosure and follow-up with you is important during this time period.

2) Medical concerns following diagnosis:

Following his diagnosis, your client won't be able to predict how the quality of his life will be. Often, the first cold or flu he comes down with is scary. It may take a few rounds of normal illness for him to accept that not every symptom is necessarily connected to an HIV outbreak.

Getting blood work done may also stir up anxiety, and blood is drawn every three to six months. Most people develop a greater sense of comfort after going through this cycle a few times.

3) When to begin taking HIV and psychotropic medications:

This is an important decision made by your client and his doctor. Considerations include current treatment protocols; adherence to taking medications, which can be complicated; the psychological reactions of starting these new medications, which break through normal denial;

and managing the side effects of the medications.

The consideration of psychotropic medications to regulate anxiety and depression is important. Educating your client about the significance of managing these symptoms is crucial for medical adherence, and overall good health. Your job is to help your client assess, if he can, techniques used for managing these symptoms or take medication, or do both if needed.

4) Sexuality:

How does your client currently navigate sex now that he knows his status? Among the issues: how to routinely practice safer sex; incorporating the awareness that there are still risks of having unsafe sex, even if he is in a monogamous relationship; and discerning whether it is necessary to disclose HIV status to random sexual partners. This last is a particularly controversial area.

Remember, your job is not to police whether your client discloses his status; far more important is for you to encourage safer sex guidelines, whether or not his status is disclosed. A good way for your client to think about this is to imagine that every new sexual partner is HIV positive. This approach encourages safer sex practices, while bypassing the necessity of having to ask questions, or providing full disclosure. Often, gay men who discuss their HIV status with a new sexual partner end up having a prematurely intimate conversation, which can be difficult for both men.

Contrary to what some clients may believe, they cannot always tell if a person has HIV. It used to be that those with HIV became sick so quickly the illness was more apparent. That simply is not the case anymore. There are many healthy asymptomatic men with HIV.

And, of course, not every person is honest about his status. Some men actually lie, saying they are negative, when, in fact, they are not. This may be the case on sexual hook-up sites, where a potential partner is overly eager for a sexual connection, or when someone is high. Men who are hungry for attachment (as opposed to sex) may do anything to get their needs met.

5) Lifestyle:

Proper sleep hygiene and good diet is important for a healthy immune system. Again, relaxation and mindfulness can enhance immune functioning. Work with your clients to emphasize these correlations, and teach them techniques they can easily do when they are not in your office.

Other options include alternative medical practices, such as acupuncture to boost immune functioning, massage, Reiki, or other forms of body work. It is very satisfying to help your client enjoy the best parts of his life.

6) Legal arrangements:

Encourage your client to make proper legal arrangements, such as medical proxy, power of attorney, and updating an existing will or creating one if he doesn't have one. It is always wise to have these in place long before any signs of illness appear.

7) Depression:

Depression is prevalent among patients with HIV, whether it is due to the psychosocial stressors inherent with the illness, or side effects of medications.

Working to minimize or prevent depression is essential. Depression gets in the way of your client enjoying the life he has, and can affect the level of self-care he pursues. Scientific studies reveal a faster viral load increase and rapid decline in T-cells with patients who are depressed. Depression is also correlated with higher levels of substance abuse and riskier sexual behavior. Targeting depression and using CBT and supportive therapy increases adherence to treatment. (Safren, 2009)

As therapists we have a dual role: to enhance a sense of purpose and meaning in life, and to encourage adherence to medical support. These kinds of interventions will greatly impact your client. Remember the significance of the therapeutic relationship. Your interactions can enhance your client's optimism.

8) Support and peer input:

The significance of having ongoing support from friends or peers is apparent. If needed, consider a group referral for support or therapy. Look for a mind-body group or an experiential therapy group in your area that teaches skills in mindfulness and relaxation.

Also, to maintain optimism and good health, encourage meaningful social and familial relationships. Altruistic activities can enhance the quality of life. One of my clients enjoys being available to support men who are newly diagnosed. Chris takes pride in his ability to help others and derives strength from this role. Sometimes completely new interests are discovered. Jason discovered he enjoys entering his dog in competitions. This is an activity he took up in an effort to widen his social network.

Despite advancements in medical care, receiving a diagnosis of HIV is still traumatic and it takes some time to figure out how to best navigate the medical and mental health systems. As a therapist, you have much to offer in the way of tools, and other resources.

If you live in a large city, there might be agencies that offer LGBT services, or, more specifically, agencies, either medical or social service, that offer assistance to people with HIV. Many of these agencies provide psychoeducational material and useful information, including cutting-edge treatment protocols.

Frequently, psychoeducational support groups are offered to those who are newly diagnosed. Typically, these are shorter-term groups that provide support and useful information. Since fewer men are being diagnosed today, this can mean that the cycles of these groups run less frequently, due to difficulties in filling the group.

Each time I have a newly diagnosed client, I find it useful to pair him up with someone else diagnosed with HIV who can speak to him about the trials and tribulations ahead. This has proven to be valuable; at times I think clients may get more from peers than they do from me. What is key in making such a referral, is finding somebody who is pragmatic, reassuring, and has useful insights and support.

In fact, there is a tendency toward peer support offered at AIDS service organizations throughout the U.S. Earlier studies conclude that peer support promotes medication adherence among people with HIV—one of the most important factors in maintaining good health. Social acceptance, reciprocal support, and empowerment occur with a peer support model and should be encouraged. (Marino, 2007) The list of resources in the back of this book includes programs that will be of interest to your clients. You are welcome to simply scan the list so that you can have it readily available to them.

GRIEF

TIMOTHY:

Timothy is a 41-year-old gay man who decides to try experiential work as a way of working on grief. As a boy he was taught not to cry. He has taken this seriously, deep into his adulthood.

His partner died of HIV when Timothy was 24, and he willed himself not to dwell on it, based on what his family taught him. His mother, with whom he had a close positive relationship, died recently and her death left him feeling devastated.

In trance, Timothy says: "When I don't feel well, I do not have my mom to take care of me anymore." He allows himself to weep heavily.

"I see all the things my parents did for me in the past. [His father had died years ago.] I see my father being supportive, smiling at me, and asking me how I was feeling. He brought me chicken soup and fresh fruit. He would take me to the doctor and give me lots of attention."

In trance, Timothy speaks to both of his parents: "Thank you for being there. I miss you both." This may not sound important, but it is profound since he previously was afraid let himself to grieve. He has just created an opening that will allow him to also grieve his partner.

LOSS AND ITS AFTERSHOCK

Years after so many losses, gay men still feel the aftershock. In the bleakest period, gay men had to just keep going. But what is not processed eventually catches up. It is relieving and invigorating to unwrap and reassemble the pieces of grief, and then rearrange all that has been held inside.

Our role is to help these men identify the internal truth regarding their losses, and guide them through their pain. We also need to reassure them that the lightness that follows this hard work will make this process worthwhile. As always, the strength of the relational connection enhances the success of the work.

LAWRENCE

"There is a long rope in the sand, and several knots along the rope representing various people in my life who have died. It is an old fishing rope. It is very thick and frayed, and bleached out. The knots were made on purpose; they are very sturdy.

The knots remind me of those who travel with me during the day. I am more aware of the companionship of friends and family I have lost, who are frequently with me throughout the day. I previously wanted to feel more comfortable with this, but I didn't allow myself to be open. I can now see a knot in the rope; I can stand up and look around, and feel who is with me. Each represents someone I have lost.

One knot is my best friend, Peter. He is quiet, off to the side, and observing. He is in the grasses, smiling, in an impeccable Armani suit. He has a nod of approval. So many of the things I do, I do so very well, and he admires that in me. I feel happy and pleased he is there, but it also makes me miss him.

He is rolling his eyes at me. He is opening his hands and says, 'It is all okay.' It is comforting. He always says I make a bigger deal out of stuff than I need to.

The next knot is my mom and dad. They used to be ballroom

dancers. My dad has his arm around my mom's waist. They are smiling, poised to dance, and they are enjoying their togetherness. Often I will see them together like this—arm and arm—and it is comforting.

The next knot is a darker knot. It is my ex-lover, Vincent. He represents a great deal of anguish and turmoil. Visually he looks contorted like a knot, always with this essence of pain within himself. Having died a drug addict and alone, this pain was self-inflicted. He doesn't show up inside of me often anymore. If he does, he is in a corner, lurking. It used to scare me, but now it is more a feeling of compassion, of knowing how I can feel empathetic. I feel very forgiving. I feel understanding of his turmoil and I know that I can accept him better than I did before. He can be with the vast array of people who have come with me during the day. I can accept his darker side."

Lawrence continues to describe other friends and lovers who have passed away. As he comes to the end, he says:

"As always, I get to a certain point where I turn around and look at the rope. Instead of continuing to walk away, I walk past the rope with the various knots, one more time. I remember to look at the faces, to bring them with me, to feel good about having them inside."

Script: Rope of Destiny

The success of this script will be predicated in part on your own comfort in being creative and encouraging.

You can picture yourself in a beautiful place in nature. You can see all around you and appreciate where you are in this moment, enjoying and taking in the beautiful scenery. Appreciate the sounds, whether you are by the ocean or in the woods. You may hear the sounds of a soft breeze, or a bird chirping happily. Enjoy the scent of fresh air. That is right. Really enjoy how good it feels to be out in an open space, enjoying the vibrant place that nature provides. You and nature existing comfortably with each other. Excellent.

As you move ahead, you see a beautiful old rope draped very care-

fully over a railing or a chair. You are drawn to this rope and you move closer and closer to see it and feel it.

Notice what the rope is made of. What color it is, how thin it is or thick it is. And as you look even closer, what you see are many knots in the rope. The knots are carefully tied by hand. Each knot is a little different from the other. And between each knot the amount of space is varied. Some knots are closer together, while other knots are farther apart. Appreciate how tightly or loosely the knots are tied.

I wonder if there is a way in which the knots remind you of someone who has passed away? They may be family members, friends, or other people you have known over the course of your life who have passed on. Describe who you see, and what they look like. Notice what they are wearing and how their hair looks. How old are they in this scene? Are they quiet, or do they have something to convey to you?

And you can begin to describe out loud what it is that you see as you look at each of these knots. Or you can insert the names of the people who have passed away at each knot.

Notice what it is that you are experiencing in your body at this moment or thoughts you are having in your mind, or the emotions that come up inside of you. That is right.

You can use images other than a knot to represent people who have passed away, such as a table surrounded by chairs, or being at a bonfire at the beach. Or, you can encourage your client to create their own metaphor.

WILLIAM:

William is one of the men old enough to have lived through the early days of the AIDS epidemic, and he still needs to keep the impact of having lived through this period tightly sealed up, apart from himself. He needs to hide the scars from the past. He began to think about his own mortality when he was about 66 years old, which was a natural developmental stage, but the pain of his previous losses was intruding on his thought processes, and an unrealistic fear that he was dying suddenly popped up. This was hardly the case.

William scheduled his first appointment to see me following a series of anxiety attacks. "I need to work on the death thing," he says.

The Death Thing:

"After my mother died, I wept for five seconds, then I never thought about it again. I feel guilty that I wasn't sadder, but I didn't allow myself to be. I am afraid there is a monster inside, something that is evil and scary. Keep the monster in the cage. That is what I tell myself."

This is a powerful image and I feel compelled to continue our work together using hypnosis. He is scared and willing.

"I need to keep the monster in the cage because as a kid, I was constantly made fun of for being gay; 'faggot' was well known to my ears." His speech is soft and his body is slumped, implying a weakness inside. I decide to ask him if he might have other choices than assuming this physical posture, and he instantaneously assumes a position of power and yells out: "Fuck you, monster! I am not going to be ruled by you anymore and you will not control me!"

It is a revelation. In our processing the hypnosis session, he describes, "In elementary school I felt inferior, based on being made fun of, and learned how not to be my true self. Because of this I became Mr. Accommodating. Needing to be liked has been the theme of my life; it is what I have lived for and I still do now. I have been living with the door ajar, not opening it up further, and not closing it either.

I have remained protected and never learned how to be angry. To this day I am still afraid to lose control. But in this moment, the door is beginning to open up a little bit. Anger is the monster behind the door, but there really isn't any monster there at all."

This is a turning point in his therapy. Appreciating how he learned to shut himself off explained why he did this when his friends and lovers had died. He is now able and willing to actually say good-bye.

We start by doing a timeline of deaths in his life. In hypnosis, he says: “I walk into an empty room with pastel walls, empty wood floor; it is a comfortable temperature in there. As I step in this room I can see all sorts of people together—Jack, Lou, Mom, Dad—they are all there and they are not sick. They all have a unique expression as they look at me. Craig, Bob, so many others—it really sucks that I have lost them all.” He is feeling really sad.

“If I only knew they were okay, maybe I would feel better.” This is immediately followed by, “I see my father smiling. He says, ‘You’re okay.’ So I move on to my mother who has both a frown and a smile on her face. She says, ‘It’s okay.’”

This is so powerful that he agrees that we will use hypnosis to say farewell to all his friends who have died.

“The metaphor of my life is that I constantly turned away and I didn’t let myself look back. I realized I didn’t want to look or feel the realities of what was going on because I had too many fears --fears of being horrified and terrified, or that I might flip out. I couldn’t look at any of this.”

Saying good-bye in hypnosis healed William and softened him. He said what he needed to say, felt what he had shut out.

One session he tells me about going to the cemetery to visit the bench he had purchased in memory of all his friends and family. He hadn’t gone there for years. “I went to the bench, and my friends were listed by name there. So, one by one, I put my hands on their names and I could feel them and see them. I could feel my feelings too. It was like visiting old friends I haven’t seen for a while. No more monsters!”

TIPS ON GRIEF WORK WITH CLIENTS:

You have probably noticed that each of these men brought his parents along to work on his grief. Make sure if your client does this that you utilize the opportunity. The magnitude of all combined losses may be why the difficulties with grief exist. It is hard enough to face it when one important person dies, let alone several (or many). You may also have noticed how little talking I needed to do with these clients.

- Normalize, rather than minimize.
- Encourage your client to use his own creativity and to do most of the talking.
- Suggest to your client that he will be able to integrate this grief so that it no longer takes up so much space or leeches his power.
- Emphasize that experiential work will enable him to retain beautiful memories, but in a positive, loving way.
- Ask who he would like to visit. Remember, there may be more than one person.
- Incorporate a future time projection where your client views himself living happily.
- Imply optimism about your client's future.

Therapists who work with gay men—or even one gay man—need to know that HIV is part of the backdrop of the entire gay community. No matter a client's age or personal history, he has been touched, even if he is not conscious of how. The effects seem to be nearly impossible to integrate. Thus, therapists need to be aware of the history and current course of HIV, the consequences of infection, preventative approaches, obstacles to safe practice, resources available, and so much more.

The first step, however, is self-assessment. We may assume that all therapists are or should be comfortable dealing with illness or death, but this simply is not true. Personal experience and age are just two of the factors that may affect your comfort level. The good news is that experiential work is especially powerful in helping clients to integrate past losses with lessons that can be brought forward into the future. The comfort that you will observe developing in your clients will affect you as well.

CHAPTER NINE
No Room in Heaven: Religion

THE SETUP

Your client comes into treatment. Religion is not his stated issue, yet it may be at the root of many issues in his daily life, even if he is unaware of this. Unresolved issues related to religion may actually be lurking beneath emotional struggles with family, anxiety, depression, substance abuse, or sexual addiction. Since being gay is considered a sin in many religions, those who have internalized this message still carry an internal fragmentation. This felt sense of splintered identity has an insidious impact on a variety of behaviors.

DANIEL:

Daniel struggles with alcohol addiction and sexual compulsivity. For years as a child, he was a devout Catholic and an altar boy. Daniel suspected he was gay at around age 14, yet had wanted to become a priest and didn't know how to handle the conflicting desires. "Why do I have these feelings? If I was a child of God, I was supposed to be the best boy. Masturbation and being gay were not okay."

He hoped that his gay feelings would go away, but they didn't. At age 16 he spoke to his parish priest, and the priest advised Daniel to focus on being the best person he could be, rather than on being gay. This was a relief for him since he was neither encouraged nor discouraged by the priest.

Later, Daniel's father asked him if he had any girlfriends. Daniel answered no. His father said that was okay, as long as he didn't like boys, to which Daniel responded that he did. He was promptly sent to a psychiatrist, and his father made him swear that he wouldn't share his proclivity with his mother, which only exacerbated Daniel's sense of shame.

Subsequently, Daniel's relationship with his father became strained, and although he eventually came out to his mother, who was not surprised, she made it clear that she and Daniel's father didn't want to hear about it. So Daniel kept himself hidden and private for years.

He is insightful about how this dynamic had an effect on him: "The cost stemming from this is compartmentalization. I learned how to keep secrets really well. My drinking, excessive use of pornography, and masturbation was kept private. I always felt guilty about my sexuality as a kid and now I feel the same. It is a dark part of me that is very private."

Daniel's observations provide the perfect opportunity to do parts work. As I ask him to explore the parts of himself that are in his awareness, he describes three parts: the tired part, the dark part, and the optimistic part.

The Tired Part:

"I feel lonely. I am living in a dark empty house. I miss cuddling with my previous partners. I miss community that I used to have, especially church." [He is sad and tearful.] "This tired place is where my symptoms manifest. I have a headache and a horrible neck ache."

The Dark Part:

"I see black. I want love to come back, but it isn't happening. I realize that I have not grieved the sadness with my father or other people in my life that I have been involved with, I just carry it all around inside of myself, dark and alone."

The Optimistic Part:

"This is how I used to live in the past: purposeful and energetic. I can do that again. I want to, I need to." [His face brightens and his voice becomes a little bolder.] I feel relief. I actually still have this optimistic part and I think I had completely forgotten that it existed. I still feel held back, but I want to face the past, and rid myself of the darkness that is not me anymore. I need an ongoing sense of community. This contributes to my darkness at nighttime. Pornography and drinking have been my only source of community and it doesn't have to be that way."

In subsequent weeks he joined a church that was spiritually fulfilling and socially satisfying, he read books on sexual addiction, and he cut back significantly on his online activities and drinking.

QUESTIONS TO BEGIN THINKING ABOUT:

- How does a history of growing up in a religious family shape one's experience of being gay?
- How does a gay man find a way to feel good about himself if he grew up in a religious family that belongs to an institution that views homosexuality as evil or as a sin?
- Can he trust that there is no Hell, and that he won't end up there in the afterlife?
- How does he make such a choice if he needs to choose between being gay and being religious?
- Is it even in the realm of possibility to be both?

Some religions are more permissive than others. Currently, there is greater promise in religious sectors for gay men. There are more gay clergy, and Pope Francis has stated that the Catholic Church has become too obsessed with denouncing homosexuality.

As significant as these shifts may be, religion is still an area of confusion. Even now, more conservative churches have no place for gay men; they are thought to be at best, misguided, and at worst, going to Hell. In more liberal sectors, the messages may be more welcoming. However, the past has already been imprinted upon these men.

You will need to tease out your client's feelings about religion in order to discern his current needs. Based on how he describes his own religious history and belief system, you can ascertain whether the solution needs to be external or internal. External solutions may take the form of finding supportive places of worship, or discovering a spiritual path that provides what he needs in his life. With the right focus, this can be a rather easy solution. Many adults have denounced religion or spirituality when confronted with having to choose between it and sexual identity. It may be that there are enough current options for your client not to have to choose.

Internal resolution is a bit more complicated. Since your client's beliefs are often deeply rooted, working with him to accept being gay and accept the portions of his religion that suit him is asking him to make a challenging internal shift. If your client grew up in a religious family, there was no way he could feel good about being gay without internal conflict, so he disowned a piece of himself in order to endure childhood and adolescence.

Gay boys who grew up in conservative religious families have more trauma and psychological difficulties than others. The adjustment to being gay can still plague him, even years after coming out. Aside from the traumatic experience of coming out, he may be more conservative than other gay men. In other words, he may be less accepting, even of himself. Some of this may be unconscious, or just below the surface. This is a form of internalized homophobia, which may result in him not wanting the world to know he is gay. Feelings of constant shame may unconsciously persist into adulthood. Living life in partial secrecy is a common response. His self-expression, wardrobe choices, or even those he chooses as friends and partners may be limited by ingrained religious dogma.

Since compartmentalization is common, internalized homophobia also manifests in more deceptive ways: alcohol abuse or other substance abuse, excessive masturbation, or sexual compulsivity, all of which may mask deeper issues. Self-loathing is at the core, and the splitting off that is instrumental to his survival may result in a higher incidence of unsafe sexual behaviors, and other destructive tendencies.

CLOSELY BOUND: RELIGION AND FAMILY

Gay men struggling with religious issues often experienced a combination of fear and conflict with their fathers who strongly and frequently advocated religious morals. Thus, the relationship with their fathers is a double bind—one that is painful. A religious father may lack the foresight to see beyond religion or appreciate contemporary gay themes. The gay child or adult hits a wall with his father that is impenetrable. The father may not have the ability to question or challenge his belief structures, and as a result, rejects his gay son for two reasons: because he is gay, and because it is against the father's religion. Separating religion and being gay may not be possible for the father or even necessary, but for his gay child, it is means rejection and pain. This is why the gay child needs the support of his father the most.

Mothers' basic religious belief systems may be equally daunting, but often the mother-gay son bond is strong enough to overcome the challenges presented or to incorporate the paradoxes of relationship. Frequently, the mother is the primary caretaker who allows her connection to her gay son to flourish, no matter what.

The challenge for families is huge, because when a son comes out to his parents and they are part of a conservative religious sector, they have to find a way to cope (or not), or risk losing their child.

Oddly enough, if parents could compartmentalize, life might be easier for the parents and their son. They could then separate the teachings of their religion from the love of their child, and then perhaps choose a connection with their child, no matter what.

KEY QUESTIONS FOR A GAY MAN:

- Which does he choose—himself or his religion?
- How does he choose?
- Does he consult with anyone, or make these decisions privately?
- Does his religious institution help him find a way to accept his being gay, or does it discourage it all costs?

***

Gerard shares the story of his parents visiting him in Chicago where he has an apartment with his partner. Though he has come out to his parents and they are obviously uncomfortable with his orientation, they find a way to maintain ongoing contact. When his parents visit the apartment, they insist that the door to the closet is a second bedroom, which they refer to as Gerard's room, without needing to see it. It sounds crazy and sad, but it allowed them to find a way to stay connected. (My joke is that Gerard really is living in a closet.)

Less than ideal are parents who might "accept" their son being gay and feel close to him, but not his partner. If they don't reject their child, they may reject their child's lifestyle, partner, and friends, all of which of course is experienced as rejection by the gay son. In these instances, the gay man has to choose between tolerating the partial acceptance from his parents, or setting limits and not agreeing to his parents' parameters, which may result in their being distant and silent.

With the rise in the number of states legalizing gay marriage, parents and siblings are beginning to appreciate and accept their gay child/sibling. My friend's father is religious and for the first time in years was able to discuss his son's sexuality:

"So son, your people with all this marriage stuff, must be happy." Nowhere near what you would consider full on support for his son, but it seemed like an important moment for my friend.

ACCEPTING WHAT IS: FINDING A NEW COMMUNITY

In certain instances, gay men who grew up in a religious environment are able to meet their spiritual needs by finding other gathering places that are more affirming. Today, this is easier, as churches (and other institutions) are more accepting of gay men. The need for community and acceptance is healing and powerful. Fortunately, many churches have gay congregants and specific ministries that are welcoming to gay men. There are gay networks and support groups within congregations, and for some men this support can be more significant than psychotherapy, since having affirmation from a minister or congregation can be what heals earlier traumatic experiences.

In contrast, gay men who grew up in more conservative religions incorporate internal beliefs that are so shaming that switching churches doesn't undo the damage that has already been done. No matter what, they view themselves as sinners. This internalization is so entrenched that there is little that we as therapists can do to convince our clients that they are okay. This is painful for therapists who want to comfort their patients.

SEAN:

Sean is a 51-year-old gay client who grew up in a conservative Mormon family. He was always religious and felt conflict about his awareness of being gay.

"In my religion, homosexuality is compared to murder, and those who participate in it are treated as such in the afterlife. My sexuality started oozing out of me. I told my bishop I was feeling an overwhelming sense of passion toward men and he told me the church doesn't accept that. These were dark emotional times because I felt I was doing wrong, yet at the same time felt I was doing what I needed to do."

To free himself, he decided to move to the Northeast in hopes of leading a more open life. However, being torn between his religious roots and the urban gay lifestyle continually haunted him. He never found ease in his choices and often feared that the Holy Ghost was watching him.

"I got tired of lying to my mother and finally took her aside and told her I was gay. She asked me not to tell my father about it. A couple of months later he asked if it was true. Both of my parents told me I was condemned. My father told me that gay marriage is a sin, and that if I was disillusioned with the church, it was because the church does not support sin. I was heartbroken."

Sean decided that the only way he could be totally free was to extricate himself from the church, to excommunicate himself. He shared his decision with his family and they were sad, yet loyal, wanting to maintain a loving connection with him.

Years later, his conflict about religion resurfaced. While visiting his parents, his father casually asked him if he would consider joining the church again.

Sean tells me, "I remember the Biblical term 'building a house on sand,' and feared that everything that I had in my life was going to get washed away."

In this bleak period Sean decompensated. He was afraid he truly was a sinner and that the gay life he had created for himself would erode and he would end up being punished for it in his next life.

During this time he agrees to three interventions:

- Join a gay male therapy group.
- See a psychopharmacologist.
- Try hypnosis to explore the use of his own strength to comfort himself.

Fortunately, all three were helpful. The group gave him the opportunity to voice his fears with other gay men, some of who had grown up in religious families and had needed to reconcile their own ambivalence. This allowed him to feel not so alone.

The compassionate care from his doctor, and the medication he agreed to take helped him manage anxiety and depression.

With hypnosis, we did ego-strengthening work, with the goal of his feeling more grounded and strong. The metaphor used: "To be able to take bigger strides."

The following are excerpts from three powerful hypnosis sessions. I start each session with a basic induction and invite Sean to use his own creativity to explore thoughts, feelings, and visual images that prevent him from reconciling being gay with his religious background.

Session One:

"I am descending down a staircase into a basement. There is an uncomfortable chair."

Since he is choosing painful imagery, I suggest he shift the scene away from darkness. I do this because I am fearful that he is beginning to re-traumatize himself. I am delighted he agrees to change the scene. He redirects himself to a brighter scene, which is more productive.

"I'm coming off some upper deck stairs outside onto a patio. There is a nice swinging sofa made of wood with soft cushions. The air is dry and the sun feels good on my skin. I see my cat coming up to me. I feel vulnerable as if something bad will happen, but from now on in my life, I am allowing good moments to be good moments."

He does this on his own, with only the simple redirect from me. This image emphasizes his ability to use resources and feel vulnerability and pleasure simultaneously. Also, having his cat nearby evokes positive imagery with animals, which is often powerful in experiential work.

Session Two:

"I see gingham plaid on the tops of jars, which are evocative of Midwest family values. They are red, aqua, black, and brown—in simple styles. The fronts of the jars have drawings of faces. There is a devil head, a bunny head, and a kitty head."

Although the interpretation of hypnosis is always unique to each individual, it is interesting how Sean incorporates his life and his struggles in this scene. His family's values are important and the atmosphere is pleasant, which he is able to see and describe. At the same time, the heads on the jars are a metaphor for what he experiences in his life: the interplay between playful, childlike nurturing animals and the devil. Actually, seeing these jars side by side is another metaphor, as he experiences a sense of relief for being able to simultaneously contain all his struggles and still feel whole.

Session Three:

Sean is returning home to see his parents again. This is the first visit since he had decompensated, due to the conversation with his father. He is filled with uncertainty about what may happen.

"I am swimming in a sea of shame. I fear more tears after that last trip. I feel a pressure in my chest, that Holy Ghost feeling. I don't want a scary religious moment where the church is more important than everything else."

Then, something shifts within him; it happens quickly and automatically.

"I can go on with my day. The message from God feels like a burning in the bosom, but I really do understand that my father's question about going back to the church was just that. It really wasn't about me, but about what he was taught regarding religion in his own life. I feel less resentful toward him."

The shift is delightful, his demeanor and posture has changed. I decide to take advantage of the opportunity and suggest parts work while he is still in trance. I ask him to identify the parts within himself that he is aware of upon anticipating this visit back home.

"There is an adult part and a child part."

The child part:

(He is initially hunched and tentative in his speech, yet quickly shifts as he speaks about this part.)

"My child part is a puppy. It is the vulnerable part of me that I feared I had lost when I became unhinged. I feel relief in having this part. My success in life requires vulnerability and I can access strength from here. I never knew vulnerability was my ally, but it is."

The adult part:

"I call this my bull part, the black bull. I am claiming my strength. I can feel it and I know it is important to claim my strength. I worried that I would lose the puppy by being in this place, but it isn't the case."

His posture is now upright and strong. I ask him to take his time enjoying this position and the feeling inside his body. He does.

"I feel relief now. The bull can gather strength from the puppy, and the puppy can gather strength from the bull. They are now eclipsed. The puppy stands over the bull and gets the attention and strength he needs. Wow. I can have them both together now."

Beautifully done. I ask him to imagine going home to visit his parents bringing these parts that are inside of him. He can see himself as the adult with these parts, holding onto his strength, making it through the visit, no matter what may happen.

The Outcome:

He went to visit his parents and was able to maintain his adult self throughout. There was a very symbolic moment between him and his mother. She was cleaning out closets and brought him a box of his things from when he was involved in the church. She asked if he wanted any of them, implying that she was okay if he didn't want them. He sorted through the box and took what he wanted and left the rest behind. It's a good metaphor: Take what you need, and leave the rest behind.

THE COMPLEX MAZE

There are no quick solutions regarding how to reconcile the challenges that come with be gay and being brought up in a religious virionment. Gay men will have different individual needs, and thus different solutions that have to be tailored specifically for them. Imagine there is a maze that has many ways to enter and exit. Some routes lead to dead ends, whereas others have uncertain paths that weave and wind around but somehow lead to an exit.

Everyone needs to find their own way, to chart their own course, and with some uncertainty, work their way out of the maze. Accepting the pain and struggles, while maintaining a sense of control, is the way out.

Treatment goals may not be easy to attain, but you can help guide your client through his own maze. The most realistic way of reconciling the pain that comes from religious uncertainties in one's history is to realize there is no solution that provides 100 percent clarity or relief. Thus, helping your client make choices that promote his self-esteem and comfort are necessary goals. Increased involvement with community, family, and institutions, while walking away from the groups that promote alienation and shame, is the ultimate path to freedom. Experiential work that is creative and utilizes your client's way of seeing things will be the most effective of interventions.

EXPERIENTIAL WORK AND RELIGION

The premise of the following script, "A Strong Foundation," is that every building needs a solid foundation. Just like core strength, a solid foundation is durable, strong, keeps a structure level, minimizes damage, and provides support to the rest of the building. This is a good metaphor for ambivalence regarding religion, since clients often feel they have an unsafe or unstable foundation. It also shores up the foundation for gay men who grew up in families where religion was emphasized over self.

Script: A Strong Foundation

Start with a basic induction. When the client is sufficiently relaxed, invite him to think about the foundation of a building:

Imagine facing or looking at a building. This building that you see is solid and strong. Notice what this building looks like. What it is made of? Stone? Wood? Brick or cement? What color is the building? Notice what the doors and windows look like. [Have him report what he sees and work with his images.]

Now, as you get closer to this building, you can see the place where the foundation meets the ground floor. This building is in good shape, because it has a strong, solid foundation. A foundation is important because it keeps this building level. It actually minimizes damage, and provides structural support to the rest of the building. That is right. The structure of this building can withstand many storms, rain, winds, snow, and frost. You can truly appreciate just how many storms this building has weathered. Having a strong foundation means that the entire building, the whole of the building, is strong. That is right.

Just like the building, your own solid foundation reinforces strength within you. You can really appreciate that when both of your feet are on the ground, and the ground is level beneath you. You are unwavering and strong due to your own solid foundation. Excellent.

Another metaphor that you can use, offered by Sean, the client mentioned earlier, involves the Biblical verse, "building a house on sand." You can provide the metaphor of houses that are built on the ocean, many of which are actually structurally sound. They are built on concrete pilings above sea level. The ocean tides can come and go beneath the house because of the way it is carefully designed, and minimal damage occurs, even during the worst of storms. Emphasize how the tide can be rough, but that each wave is different, and that the structure can withstand all of the storms that come with the seasons.

Create Your Own Script

Remember: The strength of Ericksonian work combines utilization and creativity. We need to be receptive to what clients bring and utilize it in either trance work or parts work. Using clients' leads helps direct them along the way. Clients will appreciate your using their imagery, language, and insights, instead of you telling them how to feel. They will benefit from you guiding them to appreciate that they can use their own awareness to navigate through the maze of religion—a maze that has left them feeling uncertain and conflicted. Emphasize their strength and knowing, while using your own certainty and knowledge to instill confidence.

With parts work, eliciting contrasting parts, such as fears and certainties or strengths and vulnerabilities, is very effective. You want to remind your client that he has within him healthy parts that know how to take good care of him. You can also remind him that he has a part of him that is able to observe all parts. Most gay men pay more attention to their weaknesses or vulnerabilities and forget to notice their strengths. Being able to observe all parts implies that he has access to both pain and strength, and that he should be on the lookout for this, instead of just focusing on pain. With regard to religion, help him access the parts of him that can decide or that know what he needs.

Ask him to identify and label these parts of himself, either before or after you offer the following script. Better yet, use his words that he describes as his parts and weave them into the script. Customization will make it far more powerful.

You know that it is really okay to not feel 100 percent certain. You can function strongly, even though some of your parts don't believe this. You don't need to minimize or hide your vulnerabilities. Instead, you can have all of your parts be present. That is right. You can really appreciate that you already possess what you need, and this inner knowing provides you with the truth that you can manage your struggles resourcefully. That is right. Even though you may have worked hard to minimize your parts that feel vulnerable, you can remember that each part inside you that you may feel awkward about, such as the vulnerable part or the child part is accompanied by an older more mature part. Perhaps you have minimized this stronger part more than you have needed to, and now your strength can come out more. Together, all of these parts know just what you need in order to feel better and stronger. A little strength goes a very long way—a really long way.

THE ULTIMATE: INTEGRATION

Finally, the best guidance your client can receive from you is to achieve unity. The dichotomy of being gay and growing up religious has created internal separation and dissociation. Instead, you can offer him healthier, more comfortable ways of living, the goal being integration. You can use the following tips as your own guide.

- *Delineate a Stance:* Help your client clarify his beliefs pertaining to religion and whether he wants to have a spiritual practice. He has probably avoided this topic as he felt little sense of possibility Have him internally amplify his own stance to increase certainty.
- *Decrease Fragmentation:* Help your client accept that the pain he experienced from his religious upbringing was then, not now. He can finally separate himself from his painful past and appreciate in the present how he has mended himself.
- *Make Room for Parts*: Help your client make space for parts. This is likely to help him own more resourceful states, such as openness and confidence.
- *Accept Grief*: Help your client accept that a backlash will happen. The question is not if, but when. Reassure him that this is normal and that it doesn't undermine the growth he has made.
- *Strengthen the Core*: Help your client to trust that core strength comes from being able to know and delineate what is best for him. Instead of living with ancient scriptures, his whole self will be stronger by taking self-ownership.
- *Integration*: Help your client to feel good about the ways he has healed himself. Integration is the ultimate resolution. He can be who he wants to be, and has found new, strong, healthy ways to live as a happy gay man and can choose how and if religion fits in.

Disowning the past no longer works. With the idea of working toward integration, your client will blossom and reestablish trust, both in himself and with others. Self and social connections will be stronger. This appreciation will expand far beyond the scope of religion and seep into all aspects of his life.

CHAPTER TEN
Aging Well

WHAT UNCLE PAUL TAUGHT US

Concerns regarding the normal aging process are inevitable for everyone. For gay men, many of whom lack the support of family, the concerns are especially poignant. To continue to have strength and hope when there is so much uncertainty about what lies ahead is a daunting task. Our role as therapists can be especially potent as our clients reach later life. We have the vista from which to remind them of their accomplishments, and we can highlight the rich and colorful tapestry of their lives thus far, guiding them to discovering new pockets of contentment and ease at this time.

I began working with aging gay men when I was in my early 30s. Given my lack of experience, I was surprised by their willingness to confide in me. Then, it dawned on me that it was often more important for gay male clients to have a gay male therapist, so as not to have to edit themselves, than to have a therapist around their own age.

My clients appreciate what I do for them, but even now I am often the one who is learning. I particularly love my work with older gay men. As I sit with an older client, I have the honor of hearing about his history – and his story. Having respect for one's elders is not simply a platitude from childhood, it is the stance from which to receive wisdom from those who have quite simply had more time on this planet.

As I age, so does my psychotherapy practice. I am often amused that years ago I was the gay therapist who had all the young good-looking clients who shared details about their adventures in the gay world. Because of them, I knew about the popular bars, latest events, and A-list people in the community. Now, I have installed a hand railing so that my clients can lean on it going up and down the front steps to my office. My, how quickly time passes.

But, I am comfortable with this stage of life. I trace this back to having spent so much time with my great uncle, who lived until I was in my mid-20s. In some ways he was a powerful role model for me. Though he never came out formally to the family, everyone knew he was gay. When I came out, my family already had an available frame of reference: Uncle Paul.

It was the early '80s when I came out. I remember Uncle Paul saying, "You have a privilege that I didn't have in my day, and I ask that you not tell your family that I am gay." The freedom or privilege he spoke of stems directly from the struggle of the gay men of his generation. As I am witness to how much change has taken place since his era, then in mine, and now for the next generation, it is easier and easier to envision a time when gay men will feel fully a part of and safe in the mainstream of society. I am not sure that Uncle Paul could even allow himself to imagine that.

Still, I was always impressed by my uncle's vast number and variety of friends. There were conservative women on the boards of organizations where he lived, gay male friends (single and couples) who lived quiet lives in nice homes, and various young men and women whom he mentored. They appeared to know him well, and they even treated him more like family than his own family.

Upon his death, this diverse group of people gathered to say good -bye and clean out his house and belongings. It was a generous act of community. Various ages, and a mixture of actual family and "chosen family" who loved him dearly came to do what needed to be done -- for him, and for each other.

Little did I know how much he was paving the way for me in my life as a gay male, both with my family and for future generations of gay men. From him, I learned about the importance of community of all kinds. Strong social networks play a central role in overall happiness for older gay men. I am grateful to my Uncle Paul, and to all of the Uncle Pauls of his time.

Facing Fear, Embracing Strength

Gay men know pain – they know it from a young age, they have met in its many guises, and they have accumulated intricate navigational skills to deal with it. Research reveals a high level of resilience among gay people, due in part to the skills and capacity they have developed in order to surmount the obstacles encountered as members of disadvantaged groups. (Witten, 2012, p. 74) Given their socialization and early experiences with stress, gay men are more likely to be prepared for aging than their heterosexual peers. (Witten, 2012) Sharing this research with our clients who are struggling, reminding them of the strength that has already been forged, can be profoundly reassuring.

Even with this understanding in place, there are deep questions that can be heard, whether or not they are articulated.

I don't have kids. Who will take care of me when I am sick?

Should I tell my various health care providers that I am gay?

How can I simplify and de-clutter so that when I'm gone I do not become a burden others?

Where will I live when I can't live independently?

Will I need to protect myself (in assisted living or nursing homes) by not letting other residents or staff know that I am gay? Will they realize it anyway when my visitors arrive?

How will my family and friends get along and make decisions on my behalf?

To whom should I leave my money?

If I am closer to my friends than my family, is it fair to leave money to my friends?

Should I be buried in a family plot?

What should I instruct people to do with my remains?

As therapists, we help to raise awareness around these and other questions related to aging and illness. Preparation rather than avoidance is key. These difficult decisions involve facing loneliness, fear, and family, so planning is often delayed. Besides, gay men are accustomed to secrecy and putting things off, especially when it comes to self-care.

Your willingness to serve as an advocate is helpful. Keep in mind that heterosexual clients may not require this layer of attention. Advocacy may include, for example, preparing clients for the possibility of not being treated well, due to biases that some providers have against gay men. Our sadness and anger around this reality mirrors our clients' experiences. The feeling of having to hide (again) is not an unusual coping mechanism.

It is important to be familiar with services that are welcoming to gay clients. Their needs are the same as those of their heterosexual peers, however, there usually is insufficient community support, and healthcare providers are often not specifically familiar with, or are ill-prepared to deal with, gay men's concerns. (Makadon, 2006)

You may be the only person your client has come out to, particularly in the healthcare setting. You may not even be aware of this with your older clients. Erring on the caring side is the only way to go: you take your role seriously and help him access the variety of services for which he is eligible.

A Lifestyle Transition

The daunting question that looms for gay men who don't have kids is how they will be taken care of when they are older. This question usually comes up much earlier than is actually necessary when there are no children, frequently arising for men in their 40s and 50s.

For older men, who are in the process of facing shifts in their independence, there is a need to account for physical needs, arrange for daily assistance, and plan for a change in living circumstances. These are pivotal moments when a therapist's support and guidance are needed. For men, the tendency to be stoic or minimize health concerns is common. Your objectivity will be well received and can help interrupt tendencies toward avoidance when it comes to these important decisions.

It is hard to lose independence, and the more assistance needed, the more challenging the situation. Where a gay man decides to live when he is older has wide-ranging consequences; ideally the move will keep him near friends or family. If this isn't possible, making sure there are gay neighbors or gay-affirming neighbors will help smooth the adjustment.

In looking for assisted living facilities that are comfortable for gay men, important components include staff members who are welcoming and not homophobic, residents who are gay or are comfortable with gay men, liberal educational programs, and, of course, an attractive design and good food!

Don't forget, older gay male clients may need resources for which they won't ask. Here are some things you can do:

Create a warm and open environment where you can provide information, resources, and suggestions on arranging legal matters, such as living wills and power of attorney.

Offer support and assistance in helping clients make decisions involving end-of-life care, including funeral arrangements.

Encourage contentment. Appreciating and being involved in social, community and creative activities that give back to others will enhance older gay males' lives.

Murray

Murray, a 68-year-old client, had been a successful career executive who lost everything in the dramatic economic downshift in 2008. He went from corporate big shot to residing in an assisted living facility in a working class suburb of Boston. "I moved into my assisted living facility and stepped right back into the closet."

My suggestions to have a happier life were basic, though not so easy. I suggested he establish community to reverse the isolation he was experiencing. In part, I was advising him to come out to the other residents. We discussed the possibility that some of them already knew he was gay, but were too polite to mention it. We also did ego-state work.

I have a sense that this kind of focus will help him move beyond his fearful place. He is not comfortable closing his eyes in formal trance because of his trauma history, so he does this work with his eyes open.

He is very visual, so he assigns each ego state (part) a color.

Parts:

The Gay part: *Purple*

The Happy part: *Blue*

The Go part: *Green*

The Trauma part: *Black*

For weeks we use these parts to make sense of his current circumstances, including his fear about coming out to other residents.

While focusing on his Gay part, he experiences an internal feeling of confidence and assuredness. "I need to put my flamboyant hat on!"

In order to strengthen this Gay part, he needs help from his other parts. This part can't be all alone because it will reinforce the isolation of being gay.

He lines the Gay part up with his Happy part and the Go part. He visualizes how they look together and describes the internal experience of knowing they are there side-by-side. Each part encourages the other parts. "I will no longer be in this building not being able to be myself." He practices this in sessions for several weeks. It is a revelation. And in a short time he is out to the other residents, and what's more, he is accepted by them. He even becomes president of the board.

At the same time Murray knows that maintaining a sense of happiness requires that he deal with the ugly reality of his past. Hiding the trauma is no longer a feasible plan. With all the parts under one roof, he is able to keep a place for trauma but the Trauma part will no longer lead the way. His ability to move along with resilience has taken over.

Mirror Mirror On the Wall: A Time for Reflection

This stage of adulthood is a time when individuals can look back on their lives and reflect upon how they have lived, when they felt successful, and what they may have contributed to the greater good. This gathering in of a positive sense of accomplishment makes it easier to deal with the possibility of illness and the inevitability of death. Erik Erikson referred to this level of integrity in reviewing the lifespan. Greater authenticity and deeper meaning replace the more superficial aspects of appearance and status. This is a goal we should strive for with our clients who are in the later stages of life.

Gay men who are successful in this phase often reflect on the closeness they have had with their families, or they deepen their acceptance of not having reconciled with them. The accumulation of other people in their lives can be remembered and celebrated in order to expand the feeling of contentment and peace. They may also review their career successes, the things of beauty they have collected, and their overall positive experiences in life. Many find that in the end their "road less traveled" actually was the truly scenic route, and they feel gratitude.

Runge's 2009 study on gay men and aging concludes that a successful aging paradigm includes life satisfaction and integrity, generativity, the maintenance of one's appearance and physicality, striving for personal growth, attending to sexuality, insuring financial stability, mentoring, social involvement, and validating one's resilience. (Runge, 2009) Thus, therapist and client may work on several fronts simultaneously to meet the breadth of experience and possibility.

Some clients will be able to attain this awareness easily, whereas others, especially those with a trauma history or mood disorder, will need extra help in finding ways to accept their painful pasts and create meaning in the present.

Simplify

Simultaneously, the desire to simplify life is common. Among other things, this can include a certain amount of clearing. Sometimes many sessions will be devoted to the nostalgic review of the history of a client's treasures -- where they are from, and the stories that accompany them. But what to do with these things? Being able to give them to younger friends and family members who will appreciate them will be bittersweet. You will feel the depth hidden in this practical task immediately, and so will your client, as the past connects to the present and the present hints at the future.

I recall so clearly during a visit with an aging client the poignancy and significance of emptying out his house. My seeing his beautiful house and appreciating his collections were very touching to him. He didn't have close family to share the experience with, and it was truly my pleasure to stand with him at this juncture.

Peter:

Recently, I used hypnosis with Peter, a vibrant healthy client in his 60s. He was feeling depressed, and week after week he was unable to shake it. His life was moving along fine, except that his house was on the market. He was slowly giving away his prized possessions to family members and friends, and he was donating items to various organizations. This all felt great, but he simultaneously sensed that he hadn't gotten to a piece of his core pain.

When we explore this in trance, a deeper layer of his unconscious truth quickly emerges.

"I've gotten old. I have had a really good life, but there is something about me, about my life, that I need to share. I fear that if I don't share what I have learned, my life will mean nothing. My worth in life is to leave a legacy and pass on beautiful things that I have learned about life."

Recognizing this missing piece is a relief. He is young and healthy enough to have time to work on this, and as a result of the session, his goal became a way to share his knowledge with younger people in his life.

Prepare While You Can

Even if it seems premature, now is exactly the right time to make arrangements for the future – and death is the future for all of us. For therapists, it's important to note that gay men who do not have children tend to have that distorted sense that they will not have a legacy of any value. This is part of the historical piece of growing up and feeling like an outsider, with nothing of weight to contribute. The old diminished sense of self sometimes rises up as gay clients consider "the end" just the flip side of the beginning.

It's important to remind your clients that gay men often leave behind rich legacies of which they may not even be aware. The therapist is the perfect person to help them understand the ways in which they have touched others in personal ways, or through work, or via their various kindnesses. These legacies, the ones that are not measured in dollars and cents, are the ones that will be remembered over time, and clients can feel deeply satisfied in the knowing that their lives have been worthwhile and will have reverberations into the future. You can help them see – and feel – this.

On a practical note, many people don't realize that if they do not create a will it is the next of kin who will make the decisions. If a client is estranged from his family, the idea that the family will have greater decision-making power than his friends or even his partner is devastating. Again, the therapist is in the position to encourage him to work on good preparation and good timing. Emotional readiness and practical preparation go hand-in-hand.

Considerations:

Encourage your client to think about to whom he wants to leave his possessions. Record this somewhere.

Work with your client to figure out what kind of service he would like to have to mark his passing and to celebrate his life.

Invite him to write his own eulogy or to review the accomplishments and/or attributes he wants to be incorporated into the eulogy. Ask him to think about the best person to deliver it.

Talk about how he wants his remains dealt with and record these decisions, including what he wants done with his ashes if he chooses cremation.

Most important, have him establish a will in which everything is spelled out legally. Creating a will ensures that all that he has gathered in life is gifted in the way he wishes upon his passing.

Using Hypnosis with Aging Clients

Elders seem to enjoy experiential work even more than others. The depth of absorption is amazing. Pain goes away, distractions disappear, and it is a welcomed relief for clients to return to their center, to their core.

The totality and culmination of life's wonderful experiences are automatically accessible and appreciated in the moment. I can see it on the faces and in the postures of clients. Often, they comment that this is the first time they have ever been able to enjoy the benefits of going inside in order to feel serenity. Having the ability to appreciate this allows them to open the door to history – and to unwrap the present, which can include exercise, cultural activities, creativity, contribution, interest in other people, and anything else that may enrich the Now.

Jeffrey:

As painful as it is to face, as our clients age, they feel the closeness of their mortality, and our role is to help them during this painful process. My work with those who are diagnosed with HIV has given me the experience and practical awareness necessary to be able to do this.

While working with Jeffrey, over time, I took on a variety of roles: therapist, friend, family, and doctor.

Looking back, so much of the work was related to his acceptance of his aging. The loss of his long-term partner, preparing for what was ahead, letting go of possessions, and his diminishing looks have all been painful topics for him.

Hypnosis provided great relief. The only time that Jeffrey really felt content was when he did hypnosis. A gentle smile would come over his face and the usual obsessive worry would soften as he entered the relaxing world of trance. He nodded his head in agreement to the many things I reminded him about, implying that he really was doing well. Each time he came out of trance he would say, "You know just the right things to say. You know me well."

The attunement skills I have honed over the years certainly played a part in the success of our work together, but his skills in experiencing trance were certainly just as instrumental. Maybe he didn't allow others to really know him as well as he allowed himself to be known with me, or maybe I was simply bold enough to speak the truth about how he could appreciate the big picture and be reassured that all was okay. Somehow our collaboration worked quite well.

As stated, elders appreciate the gift of trance on a profound level. The use of imagery, the incorporation of scenes involving nature, and the inclusion of mindfulness are just some of the gems that you can share. One beautiful day I asked Jeffrey to appreciate the sounds and smells of nature. It was early autumn on the outer cape where it is stunning. As he was able to do this, his joyful experience and happy smile emerged. I asked him to bottle up those sounds and smells for future use.

All We Need Is Love

Having close gay male friends who serve as family is an important norm in the gay community. These bonds often compensate for gay men's painful childhood experiences when the power and reliability of family connection was lost to them.

There is literature to support this concept. In one study, De Vries and Megathlin (2009) explored the meaning of friendship for gay men and found that gay men are more likely than heterosexuals to define friendship through expressions of loyalty, commitment, trust, love and care, rather than shared activities or group similarities, which is more common among heterosexual men. (Witten, 2012) In another study, De Vries and Hoctel (2007) found that many respondents reported that their friends are like family, and they refer to them as their "inner circle of family." (Witten, 2012, p. 102) Thus, encouraging clients to cultivate new friendships as they continue to support their already well-established ones is essential guidance.

Speaking of these ideas is one level of guidance, whereas inviting the client to take the images that come up inside the therapy room to be used outside of the therapy room is a gift that may have a profound effect at difficult times – when he feels isolated, afraid, and as though life is slipping away.

***

The following script may be adapted to the specific person and circumstances, and to your own communication style. The experience of deep comfort can bolster feelings of serenity and hopefulness. Aging well means different things to different people, but certainly it means being in accord with reality as it is. For gay men this may require enlisting resources beyond the *status quo*.

Script: Inner Circle

Start with a basic induction, and then ...

Imagine a beautiful large circle, perhaps in the sand, in an open field, or even one that has been assembled with various stones. You can choose a place that is just right for you, a wonderful place outdoors, or indoors.

Look all around you, appreciate the beauty of these surroundings, take in the sounds, the smells, or simply notice the textures and the edges of this circle. Appreciate that inside of this circle is a space that is contained and sacred; it is your safety net.

Now, just notice that there is an opening to this circle. Perhaps it is a gate, or simply a small opening where people can intentionally enter, with your permission. And you know that you are the gatekeeper of this inner circle. You allow those who deserve to be with you to enter through this opening and you do well in maintaining the protection that you need between the outside and the inside world. That is right.

(If you need the details, you can ask the client to describe this place.)

This is the place where your closest friends and family are next to you during very important moments throughout your lifetime; perhaps during happy moments, but also during times of pain, and vulnerability.

These may have been moments in the past, or moments that will take place in your future. This is the place where support is generous, just for you. That is right.

Just notice who is with you -- how each person looks, the expression on his face or her face, and how various people are situated inside of your inner circle. Excellent. You can also notice their body language as they tend to your needs inside of this special place.

Allow them to surround you, and as they do, you can experience the powerful strength of each and every one of these relationships.

Enjoy what you are experiencing in this moment. Appreciate where you feel these special feelings inside your body. Excellent. This place, inside your body, is the place that you will remember being in your own inner circle, with these special people who will give you just what you need, in each and every moment that you need it. They are with you now, and with you in the future too. That is right.

***

Aging well is a developmental journey. As therapists, we accompany our clients at many and varied important moments in their lives. We are asked to provide different types of advocacy at different times. We also face our own challenges. When we work with older clients, we get to know the inevitably of death intimately. We have to be comfortable with our own feelings about the aging process and with the prospect of death. Remember, that it is the *relationship* that houses effective intervention. Thus, our comfort and ability to stay open, even at difficult junctures, directly affects how our clients receive therapeu-

CHAPTER ELEVEN

Moving Forward— A Generative Life

BEING GAY AND LIVING HAPPY: "YOU CAN"

Now that you know a little more about gay life and how experiential work, including hypnosis, can be affective, you are in the position to help guide your clients move toward a fuller, richer life—presence unwrapped!

Since a gay man's strength can be weakened by focusing on his history and repetitive internal reactions that are no longer needed, the goal for him is to reclaim his strength. Your creative guidance will be invaluable at this juncture.

Listen carefully in your sessions. Clients will lightly or jokingly allude to topics that keep them feeling diminished. Despite the humor, these are hindrances to their well-being that you can help change.

SOME CLOSING IDEAS FOR OPENING UP POSSIBILITY:

Compare self to self. Comparing oneself to gay stereotypes creates feelings of inadequacy. Using a self-to-self comparison for growth is far more productive. As long as your client is doing personal growth work, there will always be measurable progress. Remind him (and yourself) of where he was and where he is now. This type of comparison is inherently more truthful, generous, and positive than any external comparisons.

- *Realistic expectations.* Now that he appreciates how outside comparison feeds into inadequacy, you can help your client define what is realistic. Happiness comes from being able to make decisions, based on personal preferences accompanied by solid self-esteem, rather than group norms that are internalized. Quality-of-life decisions include how to spend free time, choice of friends, where to travel, where to live, diet, exercise, and general self-care.
- *Personal style.* Feeling good about style choices fosters feelings of security. Helping clients discern and then emphasize the things that matter to them and let go of the things that really don't, are pivotal therapeutic tasks. If a client can rest in his own sense of personal style, he won't be so vulnerable to the judgments of others, some of which are probably only in his own mind anyway.
- *Incorporate community with a varied support network.* Activities that involve being social help create networks that provide a sense of belonging. Being happy likely means interacting with more than just the gay community.
- *Entertain.* Entertaining other people involves sharing and opening up in a vital way. Encouraging your client to share his home is a wonderful metaphor. Help him to let people in and see who he really is ... nothing is more satisfying.
- *Alone is good.* Breaking out of the mold is refreshing. True liberation comes from pursuing individual areas of interest, which sometimes means not blindly following community norms. Fears of being alone will abate and new feelings of deep satisfaction will take root.
- *Giving back brings back.* Altruistic activities improve mood and a sense of contentment. Help your clients assess how to share

their generosity through volunteer work, assisting friends or family members who are in need, or mentoring. It is great to discover you have a gift to offer—and it is a wonderful feeling to have it appreciated.

- *Creativity.* Creativity comes in all forms. For some it involves making wardrobe or design choices, for others it is cooking or writing. Artists who create as a vocation or a hobby feel most alive while being creative, something from which everyone can learn. Creativity can be the energy that brings people out of isolation into connection, with others, and with self.

CHOSEN FAMILY: BEING FRIENDS WITH OTHER GAY MEN

Clearly, there is safety in the tribe of those who are like-minded, yet I also wonder about the limitations. Creating a network made up of a variety of friends offers varying perspectives—about life, family, pleasure, and love. In the past, maybe my own perspective was more pathology-oriented than strength-oriented. Perhaps really both things are true: there is benefit in forging relationships with like-minded people, and there is benefit in casting a wider social net. Of course, there is literature to support one or the other, but I prefer to believe that both matter. It took getting out of the tribe of like-minded folks to expand my own view.

I support my clients with the notion of "chosen family." They can choose friendships that serve the role of family. Often these matches based on similar cultural norms and preferences are more relaxed and closer than biological families. I am delighted by the research that supports this view. It helps me appreciate the idea that gay men staying in an exclusively gay male social circle can be something positive, rather than judging the pattern as simply fear driven and exclusionary. "The search for community and care of community is a frequently repeated theme in the lives of gay men." (Witten, 2012, p. 95)

For heterosexuals, it is family who typically meet needs for affection, but for gay men, friends meet needs of loyalty, commitment, and expression of love and care.

I am struck by how my clients who enjoy experiential work spontaneously and automatically utilize the support of their family or friends in a trance state. All on their own, they find their way to their "inner circle," and use the people inside this circle to help empower their self-esteem and sense of feeling and being loved. They somehow get there and enjoy the rewards of being connected to others, either in their imaginations, or in their appreciation of the experiences they have had with those who are or have been close to them.

TERRY:

Terry is an isolated gay man who struggles with addiction. I decide to incorporate into his hypnosis session the theme of his being known and loved by his family and friends.

During trance, I ask him to imagine achieving his goal of sobriety, and how it would feel to share the triumph with those who know him well. I invite him to imagine being in a parade on an old-fashioned Main Street, where people are cheering him on. I also ask him to notice who they are.

He begins to weep. "I am shedding a skin of sorts. I am usually unaccustomed to having any type of recognition."

I ask him about the people who are there and a look of excitement comes over his face.

"I see my regular peeps. It feels so good to have them supporting me. But I also see my mother [now deceased] who always supported me. She was always a good fan of mine and now she is here with me again! I am looking for my father but I can't find him. It really disappoints me that he isn't here."

Suddenly, he says, "Good job, Terry, good job".

This is a powerful moment. Saddened by his father's absence, and in the midst of the grief, he is able to father himself. He has internalized enough care to acknowledge his accomplishment and to praise it.

Script: Parade

This is a script that works with multiple meanings. Most significantly, it is the feeling of celebration regarding accomplishments and simply being yourself. This may be an unusual and important celebration for gay men, given their years of internalizing messages of self-erasure and shame.

Most gay men are familiar with a gay pride march, so a parade in trance may indirectly connote pride.

You are on an old-fashioned Main Street where there are crowds of people lined up along both sides of the street. Look around, notice what the buildings look like, whether they are made of brick, stone, or glass and steel.

Imagine the festive feeling in this town. Who else is in this parade? Is there anyone you know? Is there music nearby?

Appreciate what it feels like to see all the people eagerly waiting for the parade. You are in the parade, going down the street. Notice whether you are walking or you are in a car or other vehicle, whether you are inside or on top of it, or whether you are on a float. As you go down the street, bystanders are clapping, cheering and waving at you. That is right. Just notice and appreciate how it feels to get this recognition.

Notice who is there. Are these folks who live in the town, or are they people who know you—friends, family or other people who have been important to you?

Appreciate how it feels to be in the center of all this. Really to allow yourself to take it in. That is right.

Notice what people are saying to you, and as you watch them cheering you on, you can take in the feelings of people believing in you, and you can proudly believe in yourself. Feel it inside.

MOVING FORWARD

For gay men, finding happiness can be complicated. There are so many threads connecting past and present, and while not all gay men have had the same upbringing, there are certain threads that are shared across most contexts.

- Growing up amidst disapproval of gay people and/or a lack of education about what it means to be gay.
- Experiencing emotional/physical bullying in school, in the neighborhood, sometimes in the family.
- Living with the condemnation of the religious group to which the family belongs.
- The shame of being "different," and internalizing images based in the bigotry of others.
- Rejection or distance from those who are supposed to love you unconditionally.
- The body being experienced as the enemy, leading the boy and then the man into unsafe and shameful territory.

These threads are almost always connected to problems being experienced by gay clients in the present, even when they are masked by other very real issues, such as addiction or depression.

Thus, along with all the other knowledge the therapist has gathered, including outside resources, strategies to build community, activities that can foster healthier choices, hypnosis may very well prove the linchpin to success.

Experiential work can help clients untangle some of those finely knotted threads through their own insights, which are not only thought, but also are embodied through the work. Once these resolutions are experienced in the mind and the body, on one level the task is already accomplished: doing it out in the world is replicating the success already experienced in therapy! What a pleasure to be the guide on this journey.

As a therapist, I have one very powerful assumption: that everyone has what I call "core strength." The core is the central, innermost part of the body. It is the place where balance and stability are first formed, and then transmitted elsewhere in the body. Movement starts at the core. Having a strong core means having a strong center. Some or all of the threads noted in the list have pulled at the gay male's core, sometimes wrapping around it and cutting him off from himself. These are the earliest imprints on his self-esteem, and he carries them into the rest of his life. But experiential work is a mighty approach, and we can guide gay men back to reclaim their core strength. Once they have a sense of that possibility, they can build their muscles, no matter where they are in life, and move forward.

The past cannot be erased, but gay men can view it from the ever-greater distance of a healthy, generative present life—unwrapped.

Script: Onwards and Upwards

This script is designed to witness and honor progress; to look back at accomplishments, while anticipating further growth to come. The title of the script comes from Irwin Michelfelder, who ended each supervision session with a twinkle in his eye and a big smile on his face as he declared: "Onwards and upwards."

This script should follow a general induction.

In this moment, you can appreciate how good it feels to be relaxed and fully present. [Expand on the ways they feel this.] *You are feeling fully satisfied, enjoy this feeling of being fulfilled.*

And as you are ready, imagine that you are about to go on a beautiful hike in the hills just ahead of you; some hills are lower, and others are taller. You have packed a bag with snacks and water; you are well prepared, so you move along.

Begin heading up into the hills at a pace that feels perfect for you. That's right. And as you climb up into these hills, you enjoy the ways in which the path winds around and around along the perimeter of the hills, moving up gradually and slowly. Along the way, there are small clearings with lookouts, and you stop whenever you choose to, appreciating how far you have come. As you look behind, you realize how far up you truly are.

You continue moving forward. You see the space where the tops of the trees meet the sky and you feel excitement about being as high up as you are. You have worked hard to get to this point.

Soon, you reach a large clearing. This is a place with beautiful views and a bench that entices you to sit down, rest, and reflect. As you take a seat, you feel content with the progress you have made and you enjoy the beauty that surrounds you. Take it all in. That is right.

You appreciate where you have come from, and how beautiful the environment is as you look ahead to the landscape in front of you. See yourself in this place, your future.

Your wishes and your dreams are accessible to you now, and you can really appreciate that what you want is within your reach. That is right. There may have been moments in your past when a part of you knew that what you wished for wouldn't become yours, but things are different now.

You can be realistic in this place and it feels really good to know that what you want, and what you deserve; and what you deserve, is easily accessible to you.

SAVOR YOUR IMPACT

The opening paragraph of this book reads: Make no mistake about it, themes related to growing up gay are prominent issues when a gay male comes for psychotherapy. Years of self-inhibition have accrued from societal and family messages, even if he hasn't been fully aware of it. The gay client has been editing himself, perhaps for a lifetime. Yes, even now, despite the progress of gay liberation, he has few people with whom he can be his true self, few environments in which he can feel fully at peace. Most likely, he has chosen to continue living life in a private way because he has learned that it is safer to edit himself than risk showing himself. He learned this young and throughout the years the lesson was likely driven home a thousand times. This has affected every aspect of his existence.

I began writing this book as an admonition for therapists to get educated, because while society has become a more welcoming place for gay men there is still a lot of work to be done. The changes in our social and political parameters have broadened only relatively recently and history looms large. And, of course, there is still tremendous bias and ignorance.

However, as I come to the close of the book I view the message as an invitation for you, rather than an admonition: to get know the dimensions of what it means to be a gay man in therapy so that you can be a more effective therapist and also gain greater enjoyment from your position.

First, understanding the fundamental truth of the opening paragraph of this book is a giant step in working with gay men. Second, it is essential to know something of the deep and complicated background of all gay men, including the myriad consequences of growing up a minority even in one's own family; the intricate defenses developed to negotiate rejecting family members, school mates, authority figures and others; and the ways in which self-identity takes shape when there is no mirror.

Third, learn more about the gay community beyond whatever stereotypes are promoted by media. Learn about the history, the current challenges, and the vital resources.

Fourth, a therapeutic repertoire that includes an experiential layer will enhance and accelerate the healing process. Why? Because gay men—and arguably all clients—benefit from therapy that offers not just insight, but a way to embody insight so that it can be applied outside of the therapy room. Feelings of isolation, frustration, low self-esteem and whatever else may be in operation can be met and reorganized experientially as clients allow new feelings—of connection, serenity, confidence—to take root.

In bringing experiential work to your gay male clients you will be offering a gift that may have no precedent in their lives: an open invitation to be full, whole, and free. Remember, the separation between body and mind is pronounced when the body has always been seen as an untrustworthy, even dangerous place. Experiential approaches invite clients to return to the body as a place of safety, strength, and well-being, congruent with the mind, no longer in opposition to it.

From one client who said what so many have expressed:

"My whole life I was so used to being in the back corner as a child and as an adult I tend to hide in that same emotional corner. It feels safer, but I also pay a huge price. Hypnosis has given me a gift. I find myself moving out of the corner into ... me! And I feel really good. I never thought I'd be able to say that."

Creative collaboration with your clients is an endlessly stimulating process—for them and for you. In holding up a mirror that reflects back clearly, the old dust and distortion wiped away, you collude with a client's burgeoning sense of new possibility. It is a continually unfolding revelation!

BIBLIOGRAPHY

Adrienne, H. L. (2011). On Fertilie Ground: Healing Infertility. New York, NY, USA: Helen Adrienne.

Auerbach, J. O. (1992). A behavioral medicine intervention as an adjunctive treatment for HIV-related illness. Psychology & Health , 6 (4).

Balter, M. (1996). New hope in HIV disease. Science (274).

Birnbaum GE, R. H. (2006). When sex is more than just sex: attachment orientations, sexual experience, and relationship quality. Journal of Personal Social Psychology , 91 (5), 929-43.

Bogaert, A. S. (2002). Adult attachment and sexual behavior. Personal Relationships , 9.

Brennan, D. C. (2012). Factors associated with a drive for muscularity among gay and bisexual men. Culture, Health & Sexuality: An International Journal for Research, Intervention and Care , 14 (1).

Brown, D. F. (1986). Hypnotherapy and hypnoanalysis. New York, NY: Routledge.

Brown, J. (2010). Psychotherapy and integration: Systems theory and self-psychology. Journal of Marital and Family Therapy , 36 (4), 472-485.

Cadwell, S. B. (1994). Therapists on the front line: Psychotherapy with gay men in the age of AIDS. Washington, DC: American Psychiatric Press Inc.

Cadwell, S. (2009). Shame, gender, and sexuality in gay mens group therapy. Group , 33 (3).

Carnes, P. (2001). Out of the shadows: Understanding sexual addiction (3rd Edition ed.). Center City, MN: Hazelden.

Corbett, K. (2009). Boyhoods: Rethinking masculinities. New Haven, CT: Yale University Press.

Cornett, C. (1993). Affirmative Dynamic Psychotherapy with Gay Men. Northvale, NJ: Jason Aronson Inc.

Creswell, J. M. (2009). Mindfulness meditation training effects on CD4+ T lymphocytes in HIV-1 infected adults: a small randomized controlled trial. Brain, Behavior, and Immunity , 23 (2), 184-8.

De Vries, B. H. (2012). Aging in the Gay Community. In T. E. Witten, Gay, lesbian, bisexual & transgender aging: Challenges in research, practice & policy. Baltimore, MD: Johns Hopkins University Press.

De Vries, B. H. (2007). The family friends of older gay men and lesbians. In N. H. Teunis (Ed.), Sexual inequalities and social justice (pp. 213-232). Berkeley, CA: University of California Press.

Downs, A. (2012). The Velvet Rage: Overcoming the Pain of Growing Up Gay in a Straight Man's World (2nd ed.). Boston, MA: Da Capo Press.

Frederick, C. M. (1999). Inner Strengths: Contemporary psychotherapy and hypnosis for ego-strengthening. New York, NY: Routledge.

Gil, P. G.-G. (2004). Long-term efficacy and safety of protease inhibitor switching to nevirapine in HIV-infected patients with undetectable virus load. Clinical Infectious Diseases , 39 (7).

Golin, C. D. (2010). SafeTalk, a multicomponent, motivational interviewing-based, safer sex counseling program for people living with HIV/AIDS: A qualitative assessment of patients' views. AIDS Patient Care and STDs , 24 (4), 237-245.

Hedges, L. (2011). Sex in psychotherapy: sexuality, passion, love, and desire in the therapeutic encounter. New York, NY: Routledge.

Isay, R. (2009). Being Homosexual: Gay Men and their Development (2nd ed.). New York, NY: Vintage Books.

Kiecolt-Glaser, J. G. (1992). Psychoneuroimmunology: Can psychological interventions modulate immunity? Journal of Consulting and Clinical Psychology , 60 (4), 569-575.

Makadon, H. (2006). Improving health care for the lesbian and gay communities. In T. E. Witten, Gay, Lesbian, Bisexual & Transgender Aging. Baltimore, MD: The Johns Hopkins University Press.

Marino, P. S. (2007). Peer support to promote medication adherence among people living with HIV/AIDS. Social Work in Health Care , 45 (1).

O'Hanlon, W. &.-D. (1989). In search of solutions. New York, NY: Norton.

Pinco, S. (2008). Is it the talking that cures? An exploration of the role of silence and words in the therapeutic process. International School of Graduate Studies, Psychology.

Polonsky, D. (2011). Chapter 14: The Sexual Challenges and Dilemmas of Young Single Men. In C. B. Stephen Levine (Ed.), The Handbook Clinical Sexuality for Mental Health Professionals (2nd Edition ed.). New York, NY: Routledge.

Polonsky, D. (2011, September). It's not only about sex! SSTAR Newsletter , 28 (2).

Polonsky, D. (2012). Talking about sex in clinical practice. Society for Sex Therapy and Research Annual Conference: Recent Advances in Assessment & Treatment of Sexual Disorders. Chicago.

Reilly, A. Y. (2013). Three predictive variables of social physique anxiety among gay men. Psychology & Sexuality , 4 (3).

Runge, J. (2009). I will survive: Clinical and theoretical implications of a study on gay men and aging. Stanford University, Psychology Department.

Safren, S. O. (2009). A randomized controlled trial of cognitive beahvioral therapy for adherence and depression (CBT-AD) in HIV-infected individuals. Health Psychology , 28 (1), 1-10.

Shilts, R. (2007). And the band played on: Politics, people, and the AIDS epidemic, 20th Anniversary Edition. New York, NY: St. Martin's Griffin.

Short, D. (2010). Transformational Relationships. Phoenix, AZ: Zeig, Tucker, & Theisen.

Signorile, M. (1998). Life Outside: the Signorile report on gay men: sex, drugs, muscles, and the passages of life. New York, NY: HarperPerennial.

Stark, M. (1999). Modes of therapeutic action: Enhancement of knowledge, provision of experience, and engagement in relationship. Northvale, NJ: Jason Aronson Inc.

Stark, M. (1994). Working with resistance. Lanham, MD: Rowman & Littlefield Publishers Inc.

Vielle, R. P. (1997). The use of hypnosis, self hypnosis, and naturalistic trance to enhance immunity and health with gay men with HIV: A contextualistic perspective. California School of Professional Psychology, Professional Psychology.

Weiss, R. (2005). Cruise Control: Understanding sex addiction in gay men. New York, New York: Alyson Books.

Witten, T. E. (2012). Gay, Lesbian, Bisexual & Transgender Aging: Challenges in research, practice and policy. Baltimore, MD: The

Johns Hopkins University Press.

Yapko, M. (2011). Mindfulness and Hypnosis: the power of suggestion to transform experience. New York, NY: W. W. Norton & Company, Inc.

Yapko, M. (2012). Trancework: An introduction to the practice of clinical hypnosis (4th ed.). New York, NY: Routledge.

Zeig, J. (2002). Brief Therapy: Lasting Impressions. Phoenix, AZ: The Milton H. Erickson Foundation Press.

Zeig, J. (2006). Confluence: The selected papers of Jeffrey K. Zeig. Phoenix, AZ: Zeig, Tucker, & Theisen, Inc.

THE AUTHOR

Rick Miller is a clinical social worker in private practice in Boston and on Cape Cod, Massachusetts. He has served on the national and international faculty for the International Society of Hypnosis, the Milton Erickson Foundation of South Africa, the Brief Therapy Conference, the Society for Clinical and Experimental Hypnosis, the American Society of Clinical Hypnosis, the American Group Psychotherapy Association, and Harvard Medical School.

Rick has been a guest lecturer at the University Of Johannesburg Department Of Psychology, Johannesburg, South Africa. In addition to his international presentations, Rick developed the curriculum on hypnotherapy with gay men that is used by the Milton Erickson Institute of Mexico City, and the National Autonomous University of Mexico, also in Mexico City.

Rick writes the popular blog *Unwrapped: Gay Male Happiness* and is a contributing author to *For Couples: Ten Commandments for Every Aspect of Your Relationship Journey* (2012). www.rickmiller.biz